Everything's Coming Up Rosie

Tim— Thanks for all you do! As a therapist I thought you would appreciate Rosie's Psych 101 - Italian Style!

Other books by Teresa Tomeo
from Sophia Institute Press:

Conquering Coronavirus
Listening for God

Teresa Tomeo

Everything's Coming Up Rosie

10 Things My Feisty Italian American Mom
Taught Me about Living a Godly Life

SOPHIA INSTITUTE PRESS
Manchester, New Hampshire

Sophia Institute Press
Box 5284, Manchester, NH 03108
1-800-888-9344
www.SophiaInstitute.com

Sophia Institute Press is a registered trademark of Sophia Institute.

paperback ISBN 978-1-64413-317-0

ebook ISBN 978-1-64413-318-7

Library of Congress Control Number: 2023931633

First printing

To my late mother, Rosie:
Ma, grazie for giving me life and for
passing on your unique wit and wisdom.
Thank you, especially, for raising me
in the Catholic Faith.

And for my husband, Deacon Dom:
thank you for loving my mother,
treating her as your own flesh and blood,
and reminding me to appreciate Rosie,
despite the mother-daughter challenges.

Contents

Foreword

by Kelly Wahlquist

When it happened, I was speaking in front of fifteen hundred women at the Saint Louis Women's Conference. In the back of my mind, I knew it was inevitable; I just didn't expect it to happen in front of so many people—and certainly not while I was still so young! There was a moment in my talk, as I focused on the Lord's immeasurable love for us, when I got choked up. I fought hard but lost the battle. I couldn't stop the tears. So there I was on the Jumbotron with tears running down my face.

Now, this welling up and overflowing of emotion is nothing new for me, for I have the gift of tears. Truth be told, I was hoping for the gift of money, but God felt it more important that I connect with great saints in Heaven, such as St. Teresa of Ávila, and those in the making here on earth who also share the gift. (You know who you are; the first three notes of "On Eagle's Wings" make your eyes water.) I reached for a tissue, and that was when the inevitable happened! Out of my pocket came a rosary commingled with a ratty old Kleenex. And I realized then and there that I had turned into my mother!

Everything's Coming Up Rosie

Looking back, I can see that it wasn't an instantaneous transformation that day in front of fifteen hundred friends—it happened gradually. Perhaps it began when I explained to my husband during our first week of marriage that bath towels were to be folded in half, in half, and then in thirds. Or maybe it started when I called one of my daughters the name of every one of her siblings and pets before I finally got to her name. It could have been when I added Velveeta to my scrambled eggs or drained a can of fruit cocktail and put it in a bowl of Jell-O one hour after allowing the gelatin to set a bit.

Truth be told, my turning into my mother happened long before I took on any of those quirky habits. The transformation of becoming like my mom started nine months before I was born. Actually, it was more like eight months, as I decided to enter this world a bit early. But as God formed me in my mother's womb, He knew the plans He had for me in His Kingdom. In His infinite wisdom, my Heavenly Father put people in my life who would teach me about His plan of sheer goodness, help me grow in the gifts He gave me to do His will, and lead me to holiness by their example.

When I was thirteen years old, if someone had said to me, "You're just like your mother," I would have most likely responded with a teenage eye roll and an "Eeew!" But at forty-five years old, in front of hundreds of women eager to be renewed in their faith, I was happy to be like my mom because from her I learned more than creative cooking tips and clever ways to make my towels fit in my cabinet; I learned the importance of connecting to the hearts of others. I learned to be relational and to build relationships.

My mom can work a crowd, has no fear of speaking in front of groups of people, and is as quick-witted as they come. Some of her traits have rubbed off on me. On that day in Saint Louis, as I pulled out the crumpled Kleenex and my rosary, I instantly lifted them for all to see on the Jumbotron and said, "Ladies, I have now officially turned into my mother!" The room burst out in laughter, no doubt because fifteen hundred women could relate!

To some women, turning into their mothers may be a goal; to some, an end to avoid. Though none of us on this side of Heaven are perfect, and many of us can point out our mothers' imperfections, especially all those we were so keen to recognize in our teen years, God—infinitely perfect and blessed in Himself—freely created us to share in His own blessed life,[1] and to help us do so, He gave us a perfect mother; He gave us His Mother, Mary.

Though I never met Rose Tomeo Squillace, I am blessed to know her through her daughter Teresa Tomeo (or T, to her friends), who is turning into her mother before my eyes (and yours). Throughout the years, Teresa has captivated and entertained thousands with delightful stories of her mom, quoting Rosie's Italian words of wisdom and imitating her New Jersey accent to a T (pun intended). Teresa has used humorous tales to relay poignant life teachings that she, sometimes begrudgingly, learned from her mom, and one of Rosie's most significant pearls of great wisdom is "Listen to your Mother." Rosie knew that to live the life that God has intended for each of us, to be the holy men and women we have been created to be, we need to follow the perfect example of our Blessed Mother.

It's excellent advice that permeates the hearts of mothers everywhere, from generation to generation. My mom, Teresa's mom, and so many mothers out there teach their children the power of asking for the intercession of our Blessed Mother. They know that Mary is a surefire way to grow closer to her Son because Mary will always lead us to Jesus.

---

[1] *Catechism of the Catholic Church* (CCC), no. 1.

It is my hope and prayer that through the pages of this book, you grow in virtue, obedience, and humility, such that you become more like your Mother Mary. And may you embrace those little nuggets of wisdom you learn along the way from Teresa, Rosie, or perhaps your mother—such as the importance of always having a rosary and a tissue in your pocket, even if they have both seen better days! A crumpled tissue can come in handy for a friend in need, and well-worn rosary beads are a good sign that you are spending time with your Mother and growing closer to her Son.

Everything's
Coming
Up *Rosie*

Introduction

Ever notice that common sense isn't so common anymore? Each time we check the news feeds on our phones or laptops or turn on the TV, it seems the world gets wackier by the minute. Right is wrong. Wrong is right, and the only unacceptable thing is the refusal to accept that anything and everything under the sun is acceptable. Our current situation is much like the title and refrain of a popular country-music song, one of my husband's favorites that came out several years ago: "God is great. Beer is good. People are crazy."[2]

I don't think too many people, regardless of their religious or political persuasions or affiliations, would disagree. And recent research backs this up. A June 2022 poll from Gallup found, for example, that 50 percent—yes, half—of those questioned about the state of morality in the United States say we're in rough shape. That figure represents a record high according to the well-known global survey giant.

---

[2] Bobby Braddock and Troy Jones, "People Are Crazy," performed by Billy Currington, from the album *Little Bit of Everything* (Mercury Nashville, 2008).

A record-high 50% of Americans rate the overall state of moral values in the U.S. as "poor," and another 37% say it is "only fair." Just 1% think the state of moral values is "excellent" and 12% "good." Although negative views of the nation's moral values have been the norm throughout Gallup's 20-year trend, the current poor rating is the highest on record by one percentage point.[3]

A 48 percent plurality, Gallup explains, rates the moral condition of the country as only fair. Those surveyed are also not very optimistic about the future.

Not only are Americans feeling grim about the current state of moral values in the nation, but they are also mostly pessimistic about the future on the subject, as 78% say morals are getting worse and just 18% getting better. The latest percentage saying moral values are getting worse is roughly in line with the average of 74% since 2002, but it is well above the past two years' 67% and 68% readings.

Another interesting survey checked the pulse of how people were feeling about the overall state of the world. Given what we've been through, including continued fallout from, among other things, the isolation and losses due to COVID-19 as well as political unrest in the United States and around the globe, not to mention economic challenges and the deep divide that keeps growing wider by the day, it should come as no surprise that those with a positive outlook are in the minority. According to a December

---

[3] Megan Brenan and Nicole Willcoxon, "Record-High 50% of Americans Rate U.S. Moral Values as 'Poor,'" Gallup, June 15, 2022, https://news.gallup.com/poll/393659/record-high-americans-rate-moral-values-poor.aspx.

2021 Axios-Momentum poll, Americans were less optimistic and more nervous or fearful about what the new year would bring. The overall findings showed a definite "souring" of the national mood, and those questioned for the survey used some very descriptive words, such as *chaotic*, *exhaustive*, and *worrisome*, for their views.[4]

We need a return to common sense as well as common decency, a good healthy sense of humor, and real joy. So what does my late mother, Rosie Tomeo Squillace, straight out of Jersey City, New Jersey, have to do with all of this? It would be quite a stretch to describe my mother as some sort of Wonder Woman whose wit and wisdom are going to save Planet Earth and its people from its miseries. But I guarantee that her key insights will make you laugh, and couldn't we use more laughter these days? They will make you think and will also help you connect the dots in terms of looking at the big picture and what matters most. And finally, they will help you obtain or maintain balance and joy in your life. I am speaking from experience with these nourishing nuggets of level-headedness laced with humor.

"Ma," as I always referred to her, or "Rosie Posie," as my friends liked to call her, was a feisty woman who, as my father used to say, was about as subtle as a baseball bat. She had little trouble telling you how she felt. Although she was not college educated, she had a wealth of understanding in the form of street smarts earned from growing up in a poor Italian American Catholic family of ten children.

My grandfather Pasquale Tomeo and my grandmother Anna Giorgio met and married after they moved to New Jersey from

---

[4] David Nather, "Exclusive Poll: America's Fears Rise for 2022," *Axios*, December 31, 2021, https://www.axios.com/2021/12/31/america-fears-rise-2022-poll.

Southern Italy in the early 1900s. My grandfather was a hard worker, but the Depression meant tough times and odd jobs to keep food on the table. As my grandparents' children grew older, they took jobs themselves to help with the family finances. Ma took a job at a clothing store. Everyone did his or her part to keep the Tomeo clan healthy and happy.

Ma, like many women who grew up in her era — often referred to as "the greatest generation": those who were born between 1900 and 1929 and lived through the Depression and World War II — also earned her commonsense stripes from her own share of challenges and suffering as an adult. These included the un-timely loss of a child later in life and a massive explosion in the apartment building where we first lived in Jersey. The explosion eventually led Mom and Dad to pack up and leave their familiar and much-loved East Coast life behind to move to southeastern Michigan. Despite many struggles, Ma never lost her joy or her spunkiness. She relied greatly on those experiences but even more so on her faith. Although she couldn't necessarily quote Scripture or Church teaching, she had a real knowledge of God's love and a deep connection with the Blessed Mother. The strong Italian American mother often turned for guidance to the strong Jewish Mother of all mothers.

Over the years, as she and my father worked hard to raise my two sisters and me, she coined several sayings, or "Rosieisms," as they came to be known — quips that became classics in our family. Her no-nonsense way of looking at life combined with the Jersey-girl accent were what TV sitcoms or comedy routines are made off. Marie Barone of *Everybody Loves Raymond* fame and Sophia Petrillo from another popular and much-loved TV show, *The Golden Girls*, pale in comparison with Rosie Posie. But there is a reason why those shows and their dominant characters live on forever in rerun land and are still so popular so many years later: people can relate to their blunt realism. Plenty of folks from strong ethnic backgrounds have a Marie, a Sophia, or a Rosie in their lives. If they don't, they want one. So it hits home.

You can take the girl out Jersey, as someone stated, but you can't take the Jersey out of the girl. One of Ma's favorite Rosieisms was "Awfa it up to God, and put it at the foot of the Crawse." Translation: "Offer it up to God and put it at the foot of the Cross." She was, you might say, a street-smart theologian. That phrase is, as I will describe, short but very rich in Catholic spirituality. It reminds me of what Pope St. John XXIII would often say at the end of another day of leading billions of Catholics around the world: "Lord, I'm tired. It's Your Church, and I'm going to bed."

Even though she did her best to impart those statements to us as motherly advice, we as kids often failed to see, until much later in life, just how wise my mom truly was. Instead, and in a truly loving way, we thought she was hysterically funny. She would often twist or confuse common clichés while trying to counsel her daughters growing up in the turbulent '60s and '70s. When she had enough of our antics, she would say, "I've had it with you girls, so I'm throwing in the table." "Ma, you mean throwing in the towel," we would chuckle as she ordered us to our rooms. And how many times did I try not to burst out laughing as I heard Ma say loudly and clearly for the umpteenth time as I headed out with friends or perhaps on a date, "Rememba, the Blessed Mutha is watching you." Again, I thought it was terribly cute and funny at the time. But truth be known, it did get me to think twice about my actions, even if ever so briefly, when I was a teenager.

Years later, when I began working as a Catholic talk-show host, writer, and motivational speaker, as the culture and society continued to spin out of control, I would often share with my readers and audiences Ma's Rosieisms, Jersey accent included. And those sayings resonated very strongly—and resonate even more so today. Yes, folks get a kick out of the way the words are presented, but it is more than that. So many have shared that they truly appreciate the no-nonsense advice, reflections, and food for thought—not to mention the in-your-face discipline that is greatly lacking in today's "I need to be my child's friend" form of parenting—wrapped in the perky, quirky package or gift that only Ma could present.

If you knew my mom, you would agree that she and the fictional TV characters Sophia Petrillo and Marie Barone had a lot in common. As I grew older and made my way back to the Catholic Church, however, I discovered another feisty Italian American, a real-life powerhouse, who reminded me even more of Rosie. Her name was Mother Angelica. She was a member of the order of Poor Clare nuns, and with only two hundred dollars in hand, she founded what is now the largest religious media organization in the world: the Eternal World Television Network (EWTN). This was long before I began working in Catholic media and long before my radio program, *Catholic Connection*, was syndicated through the network she founded. Way back in the 1980s, a radio colleague of mine handed me one of the small booklets that Mother Angelica used to write and distribute. Slowly, as my husband and I were working our way through our troubles, I began to watch the network and learned more about this amazing nun, formerly Rita Rizzo, who had so much spitfire and spunk that she plowed through one obstacle after another to do what she could to fulfill a promise she made to God: to build a monastery in His honor—and in the South, no less, smack in the middle of the Bible Belt. In addition to building that monastery, she felt the Lord calling her to defend and teach the Catholic Faith. She began with her own TV segments on a local CBS affiliate, but when that station began airing seedy content, she decided she would build not only her own TV station but an actual television network. The rest, as they say, is history.

Mother Angelica reminded me of my own mother. Both were of Italian heritage. Both were born in the 1920s. And when you become familiar with some of Mother Angelica's most popular quotes, you'll no doubt see that Rose and Rita had other traits in common. They had no problem speaking their minds and had little tolerance, as they both saw and experienced their own share of suffering, for those who spent too much time feeling sorry for themselves. The first chapter of this book, for example, is dedicated to one of Rosie's most common quips: "Awfa it up to God, and put it at the foot of the Crawse." One of Mother Angelica's lovingly in-your-face comments was "The Cross is not negotiable, sweetheart."

Another one of my Mother Angelica favorites deals with the idea that this pilgrimage on earth is not easy and that faith requires trust and persistence in good times and in bad: "Faith is one foot in the air, one foot on the ground, and a queasy feeling in the stomach."

Rosie would always tell my sisters and me, when we would complain about this, that, or the other thing, that we shouldn't expect every step to be secure or for life always to go our way. "It's not all peaches and cream, you know."

Life is not easy, but it also, as I'm sure Rosie and Rita would agree, is not meant to be lived in drudgery or misery. With the help of God, you do your best, and in whatever circumstances you find yourself, you "keep smiling."

I hope this book results in lots of smiles, some chuckles, and a great deal of encouragement and insight on how to look at life through, shall we say, Rosie-colored glasses. My mother never gave up, even after the death in 2010 of my sweet father, the love of her life, and the death of my older sister Donna from cancer in 2016. My mother's faith and her positive outlook kept her going until the ripe old age of ninety-four. Thanks to her outgoing personality, she became one of the most popular residents of the lovely assisted-living facility where she spent the last two years of her life.

I also pray that this book helps in the healing process of those who did not have the best relationship with their mothers. Truth be known, Ma and I loved each other dearly, but to claim that we merely disagreed occasionally would be a major understatement. We were in some ways as different as we were alike. I certainly inherited her extroverted nature, which earned her yet another nickname, Nosie Rosie, as she would talk to anyone anywhere at any time. We both had the tough Italian American personalities. That inquisitiveness and toughness would serve me well in my chosen communications profession, especially in my years as a radio and TV news reporter on the rough-and-tumble streets of Detroit. But the similarities ended there. Without getting into the weeds of family drama that so many of us experience, suffice it to say that our differences led to struggles in our mother-daughter relationship. The struggles, in turn, often led to ups and downs, including some distance at times.

Thanks be to God, as my mom began to age and as my husband and I grew in our Catholic Faith, we learned to appreciate her and enjoy the time we had. Even though the process of elder care was demanding and on occasion even nerve-racking, I learned a lot about the aging process and learned some new insights about Rosie as well. Our relationship was hardly the makings of a Hallmark Mother's Day movie, but in the end, we were very close, and in terms of our differences, we had learned to agree to disagree.

Since I believe in giving credit where credit is due, in addition to thanking Ma, I have to thank my dear friend Kelly Wahlquist. Kelly never met my mother, but she felt as if she knew her, and as one of my closest friends and colleagues, she also shared that, through Rosie, she has come to know me even better.

It was Kelly, a much-loved and well-known author and speaker in her own right, who wisely kept insisting not only that Rosie Posie's phrases needed to be in a book but that the book needed to be titled at least in part *Everything's Coming Up Rosie*. And isn't that the truth! Now that Rosie has passed on, I find myself quoting her more—not only on the air and in presentations but in general conversations, in my quiet time of prayer, and in discussions with my precious grandnieces Lilliana, Francesca, and Danica, who never had the chance to know her but have certainly inherited some of her best qualities.

As Kelly explained in her beautiful foreword, we all at some time turn into our mothers, even if we don't want to admit it. One of Rosie's habits that I've inherited is the ability to get a phrase, a word, or a cliché entirely wrong. Kelly has witnessed this on many occasions—sometimes spewing out her beverage in a burst of laughter.

One late summer morning, my husband and I were finishing our morning coffee on the patio when a light rain began to fall.

"Oh no, it's drippling out," I stated.

"Drippling? Don't you mean drizzling? Wow! You are becoming your mother."

So yes, as my dear friend Kelly says, everything is indeed "coming up Rosie," now more than ever. Rosie has planted a lot of seeds, and they have been fertilized by faith and watered with feistiness; those seeds are growing thanks to a heaping dose of gratitude from those who are hungry for the true, the good, and the beautiful. I pray that *Everything's Coming Up Rosie* will help you and yours grow your own garden of goodness. And no matter what happens or what ails you, remember—or "rememba"—what Ma used to say: "Keep smiling."

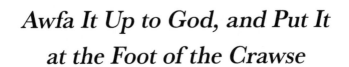

Awfa It Up to God, and Put It at the Foot of the Crawse

Rosie's version of Catholic teaching on redemptive
suffering, or letting it go, as Elsa would say

1

For this momentary light affliction is producing for us
an eternal weight of glory beyond all comparison.

—2 Corinthians 4:17

"Awfa it up to God, and put it at the foot of the Crawse": I doubt my mother realized what a powerful theological punch she was throwing with this statement. She would hardly have considered herself spiritually wise and would never have compared herself with a great saint or theologian. Saying this was her way of helping my sisters and me to learn how to deal gracefully with discomfort, disappointment, and suffering in general and to become accustomed to using bad situations for a greater good. In other words, she was passing on an extremely valuable lesson by helping us to develop an appreciation for the Catholic Church's teaching on what's known as redemptive suffering.

The concept of placing our sufferings before God was something that parents of baby boomers learned quickly, given the world in which they were raised—a world that was stricken with war and poverty for a long time. Their situation helped them push through the pain, so to speak, and to realize that although suffering was part of life, they didn't have to let problems weigh them down 24/7. St. Teresa of Ávila said, "Pain is never permanent." Rosie and other moms of her era knew that through prayer, perseverance, and a good dose of common sense, they could get through just about anything and come out stronger on the other side.

But whenever I heard this saying from Rosie's lips, I often rolled my eyes. After all, *giving* God our physical pains and our emotional struggles didn't seem to make any sense. What in the world would the Creator of the universe want with our struggles? I found myself asking—as I'm sure countless other Catholic kids from my generation did—questions such as "Why in the world would God want my stomach flu?" "Why would God want my headache?" "Why would God want the anger I'm feeling toward that rotten kid down the street?" And it was even more irritating and confusing when my sisters and I tried to offer up our sufferings, and our troubles didn't vanish into thin air, as we had hoped. How was that "offering it up" idea working for us? Not so well, or so we thought. As a young person, I failed to appreciate that this was indeed the point: to learn to handle the not-so-comfortable experiences in our lives with patience instead of whining nonstop, to pray during that stomachache, or perhaps to offer those pangs and yucky feelings for someone dealing with much bigger issues.

Ma didn't provide an official type of catechesis on the idea of offering it up or redemptive suffering. She just offered things up, day in and day out. Sometimes it was little things, such as choosing not to nag my father one last time about ditching that old Thunderbird that was getting rustier by the minute as it sat practically in our backyard—the jalopy he swore he was going to bring back to life. (Okay in full disclosure, after a few months of practicing what she preached regarding the fixer-upper, she did finally bust a gasket, telling Dad, "Either the rust bucket goes, or I go." But she really did bite her lip several times prior to that outburst.) Or she would silently finish our chores around the house on a Saturday morning so we could stay in bed a while longer, even though she was the one who really needed to rest.

Both Mom and Dad repeatedly extended forgiveness to those in their immediate circle of family and friends, something greatly lacking in our current tit-for-tat or, shall we say, tweet-for-tweet, crazed social-media-dominated culture. Since we have the technology to say what we want whenever we desire, without having to tell someone how we feel face-to-face or reveal our identity, we go for it. Fallout be damned. A priest friend of mine uses a graphic analogy for the inability to offer it up, let it go, or refrain from responding in kind to every nasty comment, dirty look, or unpleasant treatment we receive. He explains that it's akin to vomiting on a roller coaster. You feel so much better when you explode, but the rest of the people on the ride are left with your stinky mess. Think of how much better our world would be if more of us pushed back less and offered things up more frequently, as well as prayed for those who offend us.

For example, everyone has at least one cranky, sometimes a bit crazy, aunt or uncle in their family tree — the ones who like to be the center of attention and will do just about anything to get it, including trying to cause disruption. I can remember wanting to run up to the troublemaker in our clan and put my hand over his big mouth or maybe make an even stronger physical gesture toward him, so he wouldn't attempt to disrupt yet another family gathering to make it all about him. "Somebody do something!" I'd be thinking. "Why does he always have to try to ruin everything?" In the case of this uncle, doing nothing proved to be doing something very important. I'm sure I'm not the only one who wanted to silence him. But Mom and Dad, along with their siblings, offered it up by not engaging. They would nod and smile, even though I'm pretty sure their Italian American tempers were boiling underneath the happy faces as they grabbed their plates of lasagna or their sausage-and-pepper sandwiches and quietly moved to another part of the room. And what do you know? Things would quiet down quickly, and our family fun would resume when our uncle realized he didn't have an audience.

Years later, my mother explained that it was at the request of my grandmother that my parents and the other adults avoided confronting my uncle. It wasn't easy. But they offered it up out of deference to her. They kept the peace for her sake so she could try to make the most of the family festivities. And to be honest, we were all the better for it because the day had not been destroyed. The siblings did their best to address the situation with their brother away from family parties and holiday celebrations.

Rosie also knew all too well what it meant to offer it up when it came to physical pain. Like her mother, she developed severe rheumatoid arthritis. Although she was given medication for her condition, a certain amount of pain remained. Little did I know how much she suffered until we took over her care. Even the doctors with whom we consulted as her condition grew more severe marveled at her resilience. She had worked many years at a major department store, standing on her feet for long hours. And she often babysat my nieces and nephews after putting in a full day at work, even though she must have been exhausted and in some amount of pain. But she never complained; she offered it up so she could help my sisters and be with her grandchildren. Perhaps this is why Ma repeatedly told us to "awfa it up"—particularly our bodily aches. Pain was her common companion. So I could see why, in a very personal way, she identified with Christ's physical suffering.

There is a lot of misunderstanding about this concept of redemptive suffering, and I'm not just referring to my own childhood response to Rosie's words. Every one of us human beings, no matter what we believe or don't believe, is going to suffer. It doesn't mean that we ignore physical illness, emotional trauma, and abuse or that we look the other way when we're aware of immoral behavior. It does mean that, for the Christian, while we're going through what might be a minor or major struggle, we can learn something as well as help others along the way.

One of my favorite Catholic teachers, noted author, theologian, and physicist Fr. Robert Spitzer, explains that redemptive suffering means that since we all suffer, if we allow God to use the suffering, all of us are being redeemed on some level. In a 2015 episode of the much-loved Catholic program *Father Spitzer's Universe*, which runs weekly on the Eternal World Television Network, host and EWTN president Doug Keck read a viewer question concerning the topic. Fr. Spitzer explained that our suffering in this world, before the ultimate redemption, which occurs in Heaven, can be healing.

First, Fr. Spitzer explained, suffering can shock us out of a superficial and destructive way of life.

> Maybe a person has an alcohol addiction or another destructive form of life, and all of a sudden they find themselves in catastrophe after catastrophe. Maybe the family is breaking up ... or maybe they get a physical disease and it causes them to think: Was all this real happiness, or is that all there is? In other words, suffering has this incredible poignant effect. It kind of zeroes us in on that question: Is this all there is to life? And if we're really answering that question correctly, then we're going to see in a heartbeat there has got to be something more. And God then can lead us through suffering right out of a self-destructive path, right out of a superficial path where we're just wasting our dignity completely, allowing the Holy Spirit to drive a

Mack truck full of grace through the holes in our hearts and bring us to a place we never thought of before ... led there through precisely suffering.[5]

This first reflection struck home big time with me. Before I came back in full communion with the Catholic Church, my marriage and my life were falling apart. On the outside, it looked as if my husband and I had it made. We had great careers. We were earning a lot of money, enabling us to buy the finer things in life, including a lovely home, fine clothes, and nice vacations, for example. Few knew that we had become what are known as "married singles." We were husband and wife but rarely saw each other. Our career goals and our drive for the finer things—our desire to live the ultimate Yuppie lifestyle—was destroying our relationship. It wasn't until I was knocked off my high horse and was fired from a prominent TV news position that things began to change. Even though my husband and I were raised Catholic and were married in the Church, we quickly left God in the rearview mirror. My being fired woke us both up and forced me to get on my knees—quite literally. I was so miserable and confused at the time that I don't remember if I recalled at that moment my mom's famous phrase, but I did "put it at the foot of the Cross." I knelt before the crucifix in our bedroom and begged Jesus for help. I was unemployed for six months, and it was indeed redemptive. Although I struggled because I didn't know where I was going careerwise, the time off was the biggest blessing in disguise, as I was able to recognize how my husband and I needed to reorder our relationship with God and with each other and get our priorities straight.

---

[5] Magis Center, "Redemptive Suffering," *Father Spitzer's Universe*, YouTube video, 8:15, June 27, 2016, https://www.youtube.com/watch?v=9nQelVcGuv4.

Fr. Spitzer went on to say that redemptive suffering is connected to what he called the "purification of love":

It's like purgation. The idea is that we can be purged of what we might call inordinate attachment to this world so that we are seeking first God's Kingdom but doing it exactly as Jesus describes it in the Beatitudes. He says blessed are the poor in spirit. That means the humble-hearted.

Fr. Spitzer tells us that we need to look to the wisdom of St. Thérèse of Lisieux. St. Thérèse says that Jesus teaches us that we can, as Rosie also reminds us, offer up our suffering to the Father as an act of self-sacrificial love for our redemption and that of the world.

We have no idea the good that can come from our suffering because God is in control of it. God is the one redeeming it. God is the one using it for the redemption of the world. We don't know. We have to be as humble as Thérèse of Lisieux. But what we can do is ... offer that up in complete trust, as Thérèse did, as a self-oblation to God, as a gift of love to God. Just offer that pain up so that God will transform it into grace and shower it down upon the world especially for the souls in most need of His mercy.

And offering it up can do great good, no matter how large or small our sufferings. So says Servant of God Chiara Lubich, founder and president of the Focalare Movement—a movement started in the 1940s with an emphasis on the universal brotherhood of man and ecumenical unity. Her thoughts on offering everything up to God were part of a reflection in an issue of the daily Catholic devotional *Magnificat*—a publication that is part of my prayer life and one that I highly and often recommend.

In our daily duties, there are always burdensome elements which entail some measure of fatigue and discomfort. But these are the very things that should be appreciated as precious gifts that we can offer to God. Everything that tastes of suffering is in fact of utmost importance. The world does not accept suffering because it is no longer familiar with the value Christian life gives it … and because suffering goes against our human nature…. Thus the world tries to avoid and ignore it…. Yet suffering has a mysterious task; it can become a way to happiness — that true and enduring happiness which alone can fill our hearts.[6]

Every time we see a crucifix, we're reminded that Christ's excruciating death was the greatest example of "offering it up" for the benefit of others, as it led to the salvation of the world. As Christians, we know that in theory, but do we really take it into our very being and apply it to our approach to suffering? Rosie knew it, lived it, and spoke of it often. I'm grateful for her persistence in trying to penetrate my thick Italian American skull. It has been a process, but the words and their meaning are finally sinking in. So offer it up. Let it go. It's good for you, and more importantly, only the Lord knows all the good it will do for others.

[6] *Magnificat* (July 2022).

Let Us Pray

Anima Christi

Soul of Christ, sanctify me.
Body of Christ, save me.
Blood of Christ, inebriate me.
Water from Christ's side, wash me.
Passion of Christ, strengthen me.
O good Jesus, hear me.
Within Thy wounds hide me.
Suffer me not to be separated from Thee.
From the malicious enemy defend me.
In the hour of my death call me
And bid me come unto Thee,
That I may praise Thee with Thy saints
and with Thy angels
Forever and ever.
Amen.

Reflection

Suggested Scripture Verses

For this momentary light affliction is producing for us an eternal weight of glory beyond all comparison. (2 Cor. 4:17)

When you pass through the waters I will be with you; and through the rivers, they shall not overwhelm you. (Isa. 43:2, RSVCE)

I have told you this so that you might have peace in me. In the world you will have trouble, but take courage, I have conquered the world. (John 16:33)

Saintly Words of Wisdom

Out of suffering comes the serious mind; out of salvation, the grateful heart; out of endurance, fortitude; out of deliverance faith. Patient endurance attends to all things. (St. Teresa of Ávila)

Suffering gladly borne for others converts more souls than sermons. (St. Thérèse of Lisieux)

In this life Jesus does not ask you to carry the heavy cross with Him. But a small piece of His cross, a piece that consists of human suffering. (St. Padre Pio)

Reflection Questions

1. Fr. Robert Spitzer explained that God uses suffering for the souls most in need of His mercy. Who is that soul in your life who is most in need of God's mercy? Is it that troubled relative? Is it that person who pesters you online because of your political views? Or is it the one you see when you look in the mirror?

2. Think back on a difficult time in your life. What type of redemptive suffering did you experience?

_____
_____
_____
_____
_____

3. In what areas of your life do you need to embrace the concept of offering up your sufferings and laying them at the foot of the Cross?

_____
_____
_____
_____
_____

Rememba, the Blessed Mutha Is Watching You

God is everywhere, and our actions have consequences

2

When Jesus saw his mother and the disciple there whom he
loved, he said to his mother, "Woman, behold, your son."
Then he said to the disciple, "Behold, your mother." And
from that hour the disciple took her into his home.

—John 19:26-27

"Rememba, the Blessed Mutha is watching you." Isn't that a doozy?
Imagine hearing that before going on a date or heading out for an
evening with your high school or college friends. Imagine trying
to pull something funny with that image planted firmly in your
mind. Most of us who grew up Catholic in the baby-boom generation were used to seeing holy images in our homes. Statues of
the Blessed Mother and famous paintings such as the *Madonna
of the Streets* were quite common, particularly in strong ethnic
households—like mine.

Rosie knew that reminding us that the Blessed Mother was
watching us would be easily relatable and that the last image planted
in our minds on leaving the house would be that of the statue
of Our Lady in the living room or the painting of Mary in the
hallway. It was Mom's simple, sweet way—since she did say it with
a big smile—of throwing a dash of Catholic guilt into the mix; or
rather, a reminder of the guilt we'd feel if we did anything wrong.

And why not? Italian Catholics possess advance degrees in guilt. Rosie, no doubt, earned a doctorate in the subject. I guess you could say I have a master's degree in guilt.

In addition to *simple* and *sweet*, I think the adjective *sneaky* should be added here. My friends thought it was all very innocent. "That mom of yours—she is something else. She is so darn cute," they would quip as we headed off to a football game or some other event. But oh, that Rosie; she knew exactly what she was doing and knew what impact that touch of Catholic guilt might have. She was not just a trip, as one friend quipped, but a round trip. I also like to say that she worked even into her nineties—as a travel agent for guilt trips.

St. Paul tells us there is "no condemnation for those who are in Christ Jesus" (Rom. 8:1). We also know that the Lord forgives repeatedly, allowing regular U-turns—as long as we have contrite hearts. In Isaiah 1:18, we read that He makes our sins as "white as snow." And as St. Paul also says in Romans, nothing—zip, zero, *nada, niente*—can separate us from the love of God:

> Neither death, nor life, nor angels, nor principalities, nor present things, nor future things, nor powers, nor height, nor depth, nor any other creature will be able to separate us from the love of God in Christ Jesus our Lord. (8:38–39)

But again, we must be sorry for our sins. And that's why Rosie's second saying on her top-ten list is so significant. Thinking twice about our actions, even thinking about the guilt we might feel afterward, might be a deterrent to something we might regret later. For example, a few years ago, the American Psychological Association published remarkably interesting studies showing how feelings of remorse, guilt, and shame impacted one's actions. Researchers asked participants to share experiences connected to embarrassment, shame, or guilt and discovered, as an article in *Psychology Today* explained, that recalling those uncomfortable feelings was a motivating factor related to a willingness to change.

> Shame is usually considered a much more toxic and damaging emotion than guilt, one that can do significant damage to a person's self-esteem and psychological health. Yet, it seems as though shame can also contribute to a positive psychological reaction—a strong motivation to change.[7]

Ma was one smart cookie. She did not have a degree in psychology or psychiatry but those advanced degrees in guilt truly paid off.

I often recall Rosie's deep love for the Blessed Mother, and I realize that in addition to a little healthy dose of Catholic guilt, she was also trying to share with my sisters and me that the Blessed Mother had us covered in her mantle and that if we found ourselves frightened or in a difficult situation, we could always call on her to intercede with her Son on our behalf.

Ma's devotion grew even stronger after the trauma we experienced as a family when we lived in Jersey City: a gas explosion at our apartment complex. It was major news and was covered by all the New Jersey and New York media outlets and even made the *New York Times* with this dramatic headline, dated July 18, 1963, the day after the blast: "19 in Jersey City Injured in Blast; 3 Story Apartment House Is Shaken, Part Blown Out."

My father always joked that the explosion was my real TV news debut, as he was holding me in his arms as reporters, including

---

[7] Guy Winch, PhD, "The Surprising Upside of Guilt and Shame," *Psychology Today*, March 7, 2015, https://www.psychologytoday. com/intl/blog/the-squeaky-wheel/201503/the-surprising-upside -guilt-and-shame.

one from WABC, interviewed him. As the headline read, nineteen people were hurt. My family came out unscathed, with not even a scratch. What the headline did not reveal was that a few days later, a couple severely burned in the explosion would die from their injuries. My father also shared how my two older sisters were plopped in a tree outside our apartment window. It was the only way for the fire department to reach them safely. The building was a pile of rubble, and it was much less risky for all, the emergency personnel included, to retrieve them from a sturdy tree instead of trying to make their way through what was left of the structure.

My father, a mechanical engineer, had had a keen sense that something was not right. He smelled gas several days before the explosion. He alerted the landlord, but nothing was discovered until it was too late.

My parents told us the story of that life-changing evening many times. They put us to bed around eight o'clock and then retired for the evening around eleven. A brief time later, they were awakened by a very loud rumbling noise. My father described the frightening scene he discovered when he opened the front door as they were still rubbing the sleep from their eyes and trying to figure out what had happened. Had he taken even a few steps outside the apartment, he would have fallen into all sorts of debris, as the other side of the building was no longer there in front of him. He stood in the doorway, frozen, shocked not only by what he saw but by what he did not see. What he saw was our street, Fowler Avenue, bathed in smoke and moonlight, as opposed to the doors of the apartments across the hall. Again, no one in our family had as much as a scratch, even though my four-year-old body was outlined in glass from the window that had exploded over my bed.

Miraculously, our belongings were unscathed as well. My parents were able to go back days later and collect most of our furniture and clothes. The beautiful solid maple dining-room set that my mother loved lasted them a lifetime. Rosie finally let it go during her estate sale when she made the move to assisted living at the age of ninety-two.

Of course, we expect furniture and other sturdier belongings to be salvageable. But what about delicate items, such as collectibles and statues? My mother treasured a white Hummel statue of the Blessed Mother that my father brought back for her from Germany on one of his many overseas business trips. It sat on a small shelf placed prominently in the apartment. That statue not only came out of the explosion in perfect condition but remained with Rosie until she passed away. It now sits in a prominent place in the curio cabinet in my living room. There is no doubt that Rosie felt that the Blessed Mother was watching closely over us that fateful night so many years ago, and it is why she wanted us never to forget Mary's protective role in our lives as we grew up and eventually went out on our own.

So many of the approved Marian apparitions in the Catholic Church remind us of this Rosieism. When I think of our Blessed Mother's protective attribute, the apparition that comes to my mind most frequently is that of Our Lady of Guadalupe, who appeared to the indigenous peasant Juan Diego in Mexico in 1531. This apparition is connected to the miracle of the appearance of her image on Juan Diego's cloak, or tilma. Among the many beautiful messages she relayed, I always find the following words given to Juan Diego during the fourth apparition most comforting. They take me back to the days when I heard Rosie remind us of our Blessed Mother's watchfulness:

Hear me and understand well, my little son, that nothing should frighten or grieve you. Let your heart not be disturbed. Do not fear that sickness, nor any other sickness or anguish. Am I not here, who is your mother? Are you not under my protection? Am I not your health? Are you not happily in my fold? What else do you wish? Do not grieve nor be disturbed by anything.

The Blessed Mother watches over us every day—morning, noon, and night. Thanks to Rosie, I still find that idea challenging—in terms of helping me avoid sinful behavior—but the older I get, the more I find it encouraging as well as reassuring. I hope you do too.

Let Us Pray

Memorare

Remember, O most gracious Virgin Mary, that never was it known that anyone who fled to thy protection, implored thy help, or sought thine intercession was left unaided.

Inspired by this confidence, I fly unto thee, O Virgin of virgins, my mother; to thee do I come, before thee I stand, sinful and sorrowful. O Mother of the Word Incarnate, despise not my petitions, but in thy mercy hear and answer me. Amen.

Reflection

Suggested Scripture Verses

When Jesus saw his mother and the disciple there whom he loved, he said to his mother, "Woman, behold, your son." Then he said to the disciple, "Behold, your mother." And from that hour the disciple took her into his home. (John 19:26-27)

Mary kept all these things, pondering them in her heart. (Luke 2:19, RSVCE)

Saintly Words of Wisdom

If the hurricanes of temptation rise against you, or you are running upon the rocks of trouble, look to the star—call on Mary! (St. Bernard of Clairvaux)

As sailors are guided by a star to the port, so Christians are guided to heaven by Mary. (St. Thomas Aquinas)

Happy is he who lives under the protection of the Blessed Virgin Mary. (St. John Vianney)

Reflection Questions

1. How do feelings of possible or past remorse impact your actions?

_____
_____
_____
_____

2. Do you think religious images and articles are helpful in reminding us of our Faith and encouraging us in it?

_____
_____
_____
_____

3. What does it mean to you that the Blessed Mother, the Mother of God and of all humanity, is watching over you?

_____
_____
_____
_____

Listen to Your Mutha

The beauty and benefits of recognizing and respecting authority, especially the authority of God and the Church

3

*If I should be delayed, you should know how to behave
in the household of God, which is the church of the
living God, the pillar and foundation of truth.*

—1 Timothy 3:15

In my twenty years as a Catholic talk-show host, I have had the blessing of interviewing numerous Christians who either converted to the Catholic Faith or reverted, or came back, to the Church. At some point during almost every interview, the guests would admit that they went ahead and finalized that journey into or back to Rome even though they did not grasp or even yet agree with everything the Church teaches. Why? Their answer was always the same: they trusted her authority. They realized that at the end of the day, Mom—as in Holy Mother Church—knows best. The Church was founded, as we read in Matthew 16:18, by Christ Himself more than two thousand years ago. Christ gave the keys of the Kingdom to Peter, the Rock, promising that the gates of Hell shall not prevail against His Church. Despite the heresies, divisions, and other attacks from without and within, she's still here spreading the gospel, to the tune of nearly 1.4 billion members and counting. The Church's teaching authority means something. There is a God, and it's not us. And it is God's authority, as revealed in the consistency of that teaching that has proven timeless—particularly in these turbulent days in which we find ourselves—that makes the Catholic Faith so appealing to those looking for a place to call home, faithwise. In other words, those converts and reverts "listened to their Mother" or to the Holy Spirit's call to trust God and His Church. They had the humility to realize that the Creator of the universe knows more than they do. What a concept! Christ was drawing them to His Church, and through time and trust, everything else would work itself out.

How many times I rolled my eyes as a young girl when Rosie would tell me, "Listen to your mutha." She, too, was coming from a place of authority, and whether or not I agreed with her or understood why she was perhaps telling me no—well, that didn't matter. She was the mother—that's why. End of story. I needed to respect that she knew best. She loved me and had been on this earth a lot longer than her children. As a parent, she was doing what she could not only to protect us perhaps from ourselves but also to help us learn an important lesson—about the need to respect authority.

Oh, believe me, I wasn't nearly as humble as those wonderful radio guests of mine. I pushed back—quite strongly—always wanting to know why my friends could do this or that and yet I was the weird kid on the block who was left out of all the fun because of my mean old mother. Then at one point, I thought for sure I had found the best response to "listen to your mutha"—a response that would surely have Rosie shaking in her boots and, in turn, would allow me to do anything I darn well pleased.

I was around twelve years old and lamenting to a friend that Rosie seemed interested only in ruining my life with her every no. This pal of mine looked at me as if I had three heads.

"Oh, it is so easy to get my way with my mom!" she exclaimed. "When she tries to stop me, I just threaten to call the police and tell them I'm being abused. Works every time."

Brilliant! Or so I thought. How could any parent not crumble under such a threat? So off I went to try out this new and oh-so-perfect concept. *Mama Mia!* What in the world was I thinking? To say that Rosie was hardly a pushover would be the understatement of the twentieth and twenty-first centuries. Given the description of my mother so far, you probably won't be surprised about what happened when I tried on the latest theory.

I can't recall the exact basis for the argument or what Rosie was rejecting at the time. I do remember, however, that the police idea did not go according to my plan. And that, quite frankly, is another huge understatement. When I threatened to call the local police department and report child abuse, instead of trembling in fear and begging me not to make the phone call, as I surely thought she would, Rosie wasted no time at all in marching over to the phone in our kitchen. As she was dialing, she said very calmly, "Just so you know, by the time the cops get here, you're gonna be dead. And when they drag me into court, I will tell the judge, 'Your honah, it was justifiable homicide.'"

So how did that brilliant effort work for me? Obviously, not very well. You can bet I didn't pull that again.

The lack of respect and appreciation for parental authority in today's world is so prevalent that it prompted a mom in California to set aside a special day to recognize the issue. National Respect for Parents Day, celebrated on August 1, was established in 1994. According to its foundress, Marilyn Dalrymple of Lancaster, California, the commemoration was needed to "recognize the leadership roles parents have and to reinstate the respect for parents that was evident in the past."

In her original proclamation, which can still be found online, Dalrymple said the idea was born out of her labors as a parent who faced a number of serious problems while raising her children.

> As the publisher and editor of a newsletter for and by parents of disruptive and addicted adolescents for five years, I know I was not alone with my struggles. Things seem only to have become more challenging for parents in recent times. It is my belief, after studying such problems and talking to many parents who have fought similar battles, that part of the solution to making our families become united and strong is for our children and our society to begin to again recognize the leadership roles parents have and to reinstate the respect for parents that was evident in the past.[8]

Her hope was that the day would help to remind everyone of the value parents have in society. The issues Dalrymple faced with her children almost three decades ago are even more prevalent today. Think about what we didn't have back in the nineties in terms of the dominance of technology in our lives and the lives of children. A 2022 survey from the Pew Research Center, for example, found that the vast majority of today's teens have access to a number of digital devices

> such as smartphones (95%), laptops, (90%) and gaming consoles (80%). And the study shows there has been an uptick in daily teen internet users, from 92% in 2014–15 to 97% today. In addition, the share of teens who say they

---

[8] Marilyn Dalrymple, "Respect for Parents—August 1," http://marilyn_93535.tripod.com/respectforparentsaugust1/index.html.

are online almost constantly has roughly doubled since 2014–15 (46% now and 24% then).[9]

With the number of teens on social media having roughly doubled in the last several years, it's hardly a stretch to say that a good deal of the messaging they're receiving is not helping to instill respect for authority—parental or otherwise. This is what psychologist, author, and researcher Dr. Aric Sigman discovered in his review of 150 studies—a review that resulted in the book *The Spoilt Generation: Why Restoring Authority Will Make Our Children and Society Happier*, released in 2009. Although Sigman found a variety of reasons for the decline in respect, media influence was high on the list. Social media notably places an emphasis on me, myself, and I.[10]

Research shows that some ninety-two million selfies are taken every day.[11] According to mental-health experts, there has been a greater focus in recent years on building up young people's self-esteem, and that, combined with the Internet and social media, encourages young people to concentrate obsessively on themselves and their public image.[12]

[9] Emily A. Vogels, Risa Gelles-Watnick, and Navid Massarat, "Teens, Social Media, and Technology 2022," Pew Research Center, August 10, 2022, https://www.pewresearch.org/internet/2022/08/10/teens-social-media-and-technology-2022/.

[10] See my book *Beyond Me, My Selfie & I: Finding Real Happiness in a Self-Absorbed World* (Servant, 2016).

[11] Matic Broz, "28 Selfie Statistics, Demographics, & Fun Facts (2022)," Photutorial, updated July 19, 2022, https://photutorial.com/selfie-statistics/.

[12] "Social Media Narcissism in Young Adults," Newport Institute, September 29, 2021, https://www.newportinstitute.com/resources/mental-health/social-media-narcissism/.

In an interview with London's *Daily Mail*, Sigman said that this idea that the world revolves around oneself results in a growing lack of authority for adults. It's breeding a "spoilt generation; young people who believe grown-ups must earn children's respect, instead of the other way around."[13]

> Authority is a basic health requirement in children's lives. Children of the spoilt generation are used to having their demands met by their parents and others in authority, and that in turn makes them unprepared for the realities of adult life. This has consequences in every area of society, from the classroom to the workplace, the streets to the criminal courts and rehabilitation clinics. Being spoilt is now classless—from aristocracy to underclass, children are now spoilt in ways that go far beyond materialism. This is partly the result of an inability to distinguish between being authoritative versus authoritarian, leaving concepts such as authority and boundaries blurred.

Although Sigman does not come to his conclusions from a spiritual or religious perspective, his findings can be found throughout Scripture—starting, of course, with the commandment to honor our mothers and fathers. The Old Testament book of Sirach reiterates the seriousness of not taking this mandate from God seriously.

> Children, listen to me, your father;
> act accordingly, that you may be safe.

[13] Fiona Macrae and Paul Sims, "The Spoilt Generation: Parents Who Fail to Exert Authority Breeding Youngsters with No Respect for Anyone," *Daily Mail*, September 14, 2009, https://www.dailymail.co.uk/news/article-1213236/The-spoilt-generation-Youngsters-lack-respect-authority-attacking-parents-police-teachers.html.

For the Lord sets a father in honor over his children
and confirms a mother's authority over her sons.
Those who honor their father atone for sins;
they store up riches who respect their mother.
Those who honor their father will have joy in their
    own children,
and when they pray they are heard.
Those who respect their father will live a long life;
those who obey the Lord honor their mother.
Those who fear the Lord honor their father,
and serve their parents as masters.
In word and deed honor your father,
that all blessings may come to you.
A father's blessing gives a person firm roots,
but a mother's curse uproots the growing plant.
Do not glory in your father's disgrace,
for that is no glory to you!
A father's glory is glory also for oneself;
they multiply sin who demean their mother.
My son, be steadfast in honoring your father;
do not grieve him as long as he lives.
Even if his mind fails, be considerate of him;
do not revile him because you are in your prime.
Kindness to a father will not be forgotten;
it will serve as a sin offering—it will take lasting root.
In time of trouble it will be recalled to your
    advantage,
like warmth upon frost it will melt away your sins.
Those who neglect their father are like blasphemers;
those who provoke their mother are accursed by their
    Creator. (Sir. 3:1–16)

There aren't too many of us who are not very worried about the declining state of our culture today and who would disagree with the findings of Dr. Sigman or with the demands placed upon all of us by the Word of God in the book of Sirach. But before we get too haughty and think that it is only a problem being exhibited by today's younger generation, we should recall that baby boomers, as an example—those of us born between 1946 and 1964—were labeled "the me generation" because of what prominent pundits, including Tom Wolfe, noted was a growing self-centeredness. Generation Xers—those born between 1965 and 1980—have their own authority-related problems, including cynicism and a lack of trust. They lived through what's known as the "latchkey" phase, coming home from school to an empty house because both parents worked outside the home. They've also been referred to as the forgotten generation because they are sandwiched between the better-known baby boomers and the millennials, the children of the baby boomers. The millennials, or Generation Y, are those born between 1981 and 1996, and thanks to rapid expansion of technology at that time, media helped shaped their generation and their self-centered worldview. There really is, it says in Ecclesiastes, "nothing new under the sun." Although each generation has its own challenges and media saturation is at an all-time high, human nature stays the same.

> What profit have we from all the toil
> which we toil at under the sun?
> One generation departs and another generation comes,
> but the world forever stays.
> The sun rises and the sun sets;
> then it presses on to the place where it rises.
> Shifting south, then north,

back and forth shifts the wind, constantly shifting its
    course.
All rivers flow to the sea,
yet never does the sea become full.
To the place where they flow,
the rivers continue to flow.
All things are wearisome,
too wearisome for words.
The eye is not satisfied by seeing
nor has the ear enough of hearing.
What has been, that will be; what has been done, that
    will be done.
Nothing is new under the sun! (Eccles. 1:3–9)

Some may find the words of Ecclesiastes depressing, as it seems
we keep going around in circles and never learn. I tend to see them
as heartening. Scripture scholars believe that the book was written
around 935 BC. More than two thousand years later, God is still
giving His children a chance to begin again—to recognize that His
authority is given to us out of love.

St. Paul reminded Timothy of this point after he left him
in charge of the Church in Ephesus. Paul stressed that there is
clear direction for those looking to follow Christ: they need to
look to the authority of the Church. "If I should be delayed, you
should know how to behave in the household of God, which is
the church of the living God, the pillar and foundation of truth"
(1 Tim. 3:15).

We will close this chapter with a very fitting story from my as-
sociate pastor, Fr. Andrew Dawson, in the Archdiocese of Detroit.
During his homily on the feast of the Assumption of Mary, August
15, 2022, he shared a powerful memory regarding the wisdom of

listening to our mother. The story related to the Blessed Mother, his own mother, and the Catholic Church.

As a child, he loved climbing a large tree behind his house. But one day his mom specifically told him, "Don't climb the tree today." He didn't ask why, but she was very firm in her direction not to climb the tree that day. He would often get scraped up during his climbing escapades, but he had never fallen out of the tree.

"Now, I would argue that I didn't fall out of it that day either. My mom would disagree," Fr. Andrew explained. "I kind of slithered out of it, down the trunk, and quickly. But it was okay, as I used my face as a break to slow the slither, so I didn't break anything."

His mother, however, didn't see it quite the same way. And he soon found out why she didn't want him to go climbing.

"Looking at the large bloody scrape all down my face, she reminded me that the next day was school photo day. So I had my fifth-grade photo taken sporting my marks of adventure."

His mother decided to switch things up a bit when it came time to get copies of his school photo that year. Instead of the usual 5x7, she ordered the 8x10, the 5x7, and the 4x6. She not only framed one for the wall but sent them to many relatives and even some people who weren't relatives.

"Mom, why did you get all these photos? Did you have to put that on the wall?"

"Oh yes," his mother exclaimed. "Yes, I did because now you will always remember to listen to your mother."

Fr. Andrew told parishioners that the photo is still on the wall. He likened that experience to the Blessed Mother's warning us to stay out of the tree, the tree that Eve failed to avoid in the Garden of Eden, the tree that got us all into trouble.

"The Blessed Mother shows us by example, by her life, her faith, her obedience, her generosity—by her love—the way to one day join her and her Son in Heaven."

Whether it is Rosie's simple "listen to your mutha," the solid same advice from another mother trying to get her son to pay attention, or the infallible Word of God providing clear and repeated instruction, it is a message that echoed through the ages. Pondering those words made me realize that Rosie was doing her best to help me understand that it isn't only our earthly parents, as St. Paul points out, who required our attention and obedience. If we can appreciate the importance of showing respect to authority here on earth, including the important role of parents, we should reflect upon how we show respect for Christ and the Catholic Church.

"Whatever you do," Fr. Andrew stressed, "listen to your mother."

Let Us Pray

Litany of the Blessed Virgin Mary

Lord, have mercy on us,
Christ, have mercy on us.
Lord, have mercy on us. Christ, hear us.
Christ, graciously hear us.
God the Father of heaven, *have mercy on us.*
God the Son, Redeemer of the World, *have mercy on us.*
God the Holy Spirit, *have mercy on us.*
Holy Trinity, one God, *have mercy on us.*
Holy Mary, *pray for us.*
Holy Mother of God, *pray for us.*
Holy Virgin of virgins, *pray for us.*
Mother of Christ, *pray for us.*
Mother of Divine Grace, *pray for us.*
Mother most pure, *pray for us.*
Mother most chaste, *pray for us.*
Mother inviolate, *pray for us.*
Mother undefiled, *pray for us.*
Mother most amiable, *pray for us.*
Mother most admirable, *pray for us.*
Mother of good counsel, *pray for us.*
Mother of our Creator, *pray for us.*
Mother of our Savior, *pray for us.*
Virgin most prudent, *pray for us.*
Virgin most venerable, *pray for us.*
Virgin most renowned, *pray for us.*
Virgin most powerful, *pray for us.*

Virgin most merciful, *pray for us.*

Virgin most faithful, *pray for us.*

Mirror of justice, *pray for us.*

Seat of wisdom, *pray for us.*

Cause of our joy, *pray for us.*

Spiritual vessel, *pray for us.*

Vessel of honor, *pray for us.*

Singular vessel of devotion, *pray for us.*

Mystical rose, *pray for us.*

Tower of David, *pray for us.*

Tower of ivory, *pray for us.*

House of gold, *pray for us.*

Ark of the covenant, *pray for us.*

Gate of heaven, *pray for us.*

Morning star, *pray for us.*

Health of the sick, *pray for us.*

Refuge of sinners, *pray for us.*

Comforter of the afflicted, *pray for us.*

Help of Christians, *pray for us.*

Queen of Angels, *pray for us.*

Queen of Patriarchs, *pray for us.*

Queen of Prophets, *pray for us.*

Queen of Apostles, *pray for us.*

Queen of Martyrs, *pray for us.*

Queen of Confessors, *pray for us.*

Queen of Virgins, *pray for us.*

Queen of all Saints, *pray for us.*

Queen conceived without original sin, *pray for us.*

Queen assumed into heaven, *pray for us.*

Queen of the most holy Rosary, *pray for us.*

Queen of Peace, *pray for us.*

Lamb of God, who takes away the sins of the world,
   spare us, O Lord.

Lamb of God, who takes away the sins of the world,
   graciously hear us, O Lord.

Lamb of God, who takes away the sins of the world,
   have mercy on us.

Grant we beseech Thee, O Lord God, that we, Thy servants, may enjoy perpetual health of mind and body and, by the glorious intercession of the blessed Mary, ever Virgin, be delivered from present sorrow and enjoy eternal gladness. Through Christ our Lord. Amen.

Reflection

Suggested Scripture Verses

Honor your father and your mother. (Exod. 20:12)

If I should be delayed, you should know how to behave in the household of God, which is the church of the living God, the pillar and foundation of truth. (1 Tim. 3:15)

For the Lord sets a father in honor over his children and confirms a mother's authority over her sons. Those who honor their father atone for sins; they store up riches who respect their mother. (Sir. 3:2–4)

I would not believe in the Gospel if the authority of the Catholic Church did not move me to do so. (St. Augustine)

I will go peaceably and firmly to the Catholic Church: for if faith is so important to our salvation, I will seek it where true faith first began, seek it among those who received it from God Himself. (St. Elizabeth Ann Seton)

Hold firmly that our faith is identical with that of the ancients. Deny this, and you dissolve the unity of the Church. (St. Thomas Aquinas)

Reflection Questions

1. What does "listen to your mother" mean to you in terms of your relationship with God and the Church?

_____

_____

_____

_____

2. Do you trust and respect the authority of the Catholic Church, or do you believe there are teachings you may set aside?

_____

_____

_____

_____

3. What role does the Blessed Mother play in your Christian walk? How might you grow closer to her in order to grow closer to Christ?

_____

_____

_____

_____

_____

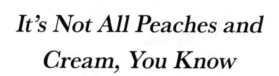

It's Not All Peaches and Cream, You Know

In this world we will face challenges, but if we
turn to God, it makes all the difference

4

After you have suffered a little while, the God of all
grace, who has called you to his eternal glory in Christ,
will himself restore, establish, and strengthen you.

—1 Peter 5:10, RSVCE

"All sunshine makes a desert." That statement was spoken by my Bible-study leader in the early 1990s in a lesson on suffering. When she said it, what sprang to my mind immediately were the words not only of Rosie but of her mother, my grandmother Anna Tomeo: "It's not all peaches and cream, you know."

Grandma shared those words with me the morning of my wedding day, September 16, 1983. She was not strong enough to travel from New Jersey for the big day but wanted to wish Dominick and me well and let us know we were in her prayers.

"It's not all peaches and cream, you know. He is going to drive you crazy at times. There will be good times and bad times and little things, such as the dirty socks on the floor, that will get on your nerves, and the big things, such as disappointments and challenges, that will stretch you and test you. But if you truly love each other, it will all work out and it will all be worth it."

I smiled as she chatted with me; I had heard the peaches-and-cream line many times, but I didn't realize that Rosie had picked it up from her mother. Here we are, decades later, and I am sharing that thought not only with family and friends but with many of my readers and radio listeners.

Grandma Tomeo passed on great advice to my mother and to me, and not only about the ups and downs of married life. Certainly, those words were profoundly applicable when my husband and I were working through our issues. We struggled to learn from our mistakes and grow closer to Christ and to each other. It certainly wasn't all peaches and cream. Grandma was also handing down straightforward guidance on life in general. We're all going to struggle and suffer at times in our lives. In addition to offering up our pain in redemptive suffering—as we learned earlier—are we learning and growing from the problems we encounter? And when we look back, do we see how God was with us through it all?

As Christians, we generally understand that we live in a fallen and quite imperfect and troubled world. Jesus tells us, "In the world you have tribulation; but be of good cheer, I have overcome the world" (John 16:33). If you go to church on a regular basis, you're no stranger to Jesus' instruction to His followers: "Take up your cross and follow me" (see, e.g., Matt. 16:24). This message is repeated so often that it must be a pretty important point that the Lord is trying to make. And how many hit singles or best sellers were built on similar notions? But it's very different when it's our own crosses or troubles.

Too often in my Christian walk, I saw these verses as very ominous and discouraging. They made me so comfortable at times that whenever I came across them during Mass or prayer time, I felt as if I needed to look around the corner for the bad guy or the bad news to show up. That's not how Jesus wants us to feel. Quite the opposite.

Let's go back to that quote from my Bible-study leader: all sunshine makes a desert. It's apparently an old Arab proverb. But it is also drenched in Christian spirituality, and for people like me, who love the sun and summer, it resonates. Perhaps it's my Southern Italian heritage, but I have always been drawn to the warm weather. My husband and I try to escape to Florida or Italy as often as we can during the long Michigan winters to avoid the cold and, even more so, the gray, gloomy skies that can hover over the northern states for months on end with barely a ray of sunshine breaking through. The long winters and late springs mean snow, sleet, rain, and very little sun. As welcoming as those warmer and sunnier places are, they wouldn't be as lovely and pleasant if they didn't have regular periods of rain showers and thunderstorms to make those palm trees and birds of paradise grow. I'm not a meteorologist, nor do I play one on TV, but prolonged periods of extreme sunshine, or all sunshine, as that Arab proverb states, would certainly lead to dangerous conditions, perhaps even a drought.

Look no further than Europe during the summer of 2022. In Germany, for example, the water levels of the Rhine dropped to such low levels that shipping was greatly impacted. And the Danube, as a *New York Times* article explained, was so depleted by drought that it revealed shipwrecks, relics, and even bombs sunk or left behind at the end of World War II.

> From the depths of the mighty Danube River, the hulking wrecks of more than a dozen German World War II ships have risen once again, exposed by a drought that has starved Europe's rivers and led to some of the lowest water levels of the past century.
>
> The exposed wrecks had been on the river's bottom for nearly eight decades and emerge only when the water level is extremely low. An extraordinarily hot and dry summer rippling across Europe has dropped water levels precipitously,

creating a hazard for local river transport and fishing on the Danube.

More broadly, the scorching weather has caused alarm across the continent as heat waves have increased at a faster rate, with scientists pointing to global warming and other factors as playing major roles.[14]

In Italy, a state of emergency was declared in the middle of the summer. In France, the prime minister called the conditions the worst dry spell in history. Overall, the extended heat waves in the summer of 2022 resulted in what experts claimed was the worst drought Europe had seen in five hundred years. In the case of Europe, all that sunshine turned the continent quite literally into a desert.

The same can happen to us. Not much grows during a drought or in the middle of a desert. Nor do we grow when everything constantly goes our way or when we expect the world and the people in it to conform to our every whim, desire, and expectation. It's adversity that really makes us stronger, if we choose to learn from it and to see that if God brings us to it, He will also bring us through it.

Don't believe me? Well, maybe you'll believe the experts—as in the researchers who studied the positive effects of adversity. What I find most interesting is that those studies do not come at the topic of adversity or suffering from a Christian or religious perspective. Even so, the research backs up what Jesus and the Church teach about learning from our challenges.

For example, Dr. Mark Seery, a professor of psychology at the University at Buffalo, and several colleagues released a report a few

[14] Christopher F. Schuetze, "Europe's Rivers, Starved by Drought, Reveal Shipwrecks, Relics and Bombs," *New York Times*, August 23, 2022.

years ago involving some twenty-three hundred participants and their experiences with adversity. Those who took part admitted that a moderate amount of hardship led to a higher life satisfaction along with better mental health. Those challenges also helped them become more resilient and more empathetic.

Case in point: plenty of us have heard of post-traumatic stress disorder, or PTSD. But how many of us are familiar with post-traumatic growth, or PTG? According to the American Psychological Association (APA), PTG is defined as a positive transformation after trauma. As the APA explains, there is a post-traumatic growth inventory that looks for positive growth in a number of areas including:

- appreciation of life
- relationships with others
- new possibilities in life
- personal strength
- spiritual change[15]

When I review that inventory list, I think of my parents and what that terrible explosion taught them about the sacredness of life, the importance of family, and their interest in embracing new opportunities, or "new possibilities in life" — we moved to Michigan not long after the explosion. And last, but certainly not least, they experienced a deeper appreciation of their faith, as in a "spiritual change." They were much more aware of the power of prayer and the intercession of the saints, with the intercession of the Blessed Mother at the top of the list.

Are you beginning to see a pattern here? Do you see how the Lord can make Limoncello out of the lemons in our lives if we

---

[15] Lorna Collier, "Growth after Trauma," *Monitor on Psychology* 47, no. 10 (November 2016), American Psychological Association, https://www.apa.org/monitor/2016/11/growth-trauma.

allow Him to do so? No matter where we begin reading in the Bible, this pattern or theme is one of the most prominent:

> All things work for good for those who love God, who are called according to his purpose. (Rom. 8:28)

> This momentary light affliction is producing for us an eternal weight of glory beyond all comparison. (2 Cor. 4:17)

> Blessed is the man who endures trial, for when he has stood the test he will receive the crown of life which God has promised to those who love him. (James 1:12)

These are just a few examples from the New Testament. The Bible, from beginning to end, is overflowing with encouraging verses that help us see how we can come out of our trials as conquerors—believers who are hopefully more empathic to those who may have experienced similar trials.

This thought was made clear to me a few years ago, when I was working in secular media. Although my husband and I had healed our marriage, I was still going through a turning point in my career. After I was fired from my first prominent TV news position, the Lord eventually led me back into broadcast journalism. So I naturally thought He wanted me to bloom right where He had me planted. The blooming was nice while it lasted, but it didn't last long. My husband and I were all in for Jesus and the Church. We were very involved in our parish. We read Scripture, attended conferences, and even took our first pilgrimage to the Holy Land. I slowly realized, however, that the closer I grew to God, the more estranged I felt from my colleagues and my chosen profession. The frenetic newsrooms that had been my work home for nearly twenty years now felt foreign to me. God was opening my eyes to the many issues occurring in the secular media. It's not that they weren't there before. It's just that I didn't see them, or I chose to ignore them. Perhaps it was a little of both. It was a very confusing time.

After my husband and I returned to the Church and after the Lord put me back on the air as a news reporter at one of the most prominent TV stations in the Midwest, estranged was not what I expected to feel. I was struggling with the ugliness of the news business, which was losing its soul for the sake of profit and extreme agendas. What could I do about the erosion of the media? Was I supposed to do anything besides try to do my best in my work? Then I heard what I felt were prophetic words, coming from a popular Evangelical author and preacher, Joyce Meyer. Her programs were carried on the local Christian station that I listened to often on my thirty-minute-plus commute home. That fateful night, she was talking about not just getting through suffering but putting that suffering to use for the sake of others: "Let your misery be your ministry."

I almost drove off the road. Those words made sense to me. Deep down, at that moment, I knew that God somehow meant them for me. My years in the trenches as a radio and TV reporter were not in vain. God had something else in mind for me. Little did I know that it would involve using my skills to promote the gospel and the teachings of the Church and helping Catholics and other concerned citizens understand the importance of critical thinking when it comes to the media. I had no idea that I would be writing books and lecturing on media bias, violence in the media, and many other media issues impacting our world today. But I had a strong sense that God would show me in time. It was several years before my "new possibility" began to unfold, but that night, alone in my car, I knew there was a light at the end of the tunnel.

Everything's Coming Up Rosie

Think about how many ministries or organizations were founded by people who wanted to prevent others from going through a difficulty that they had gone through; those who believed that a problem could be solved more efficiently. Two recovering alcoholics, Bill Wilson and Dr. Robert Smith, founded Alcoholics Anonymous (AA) in 1935. Today there are more than sixty thousand chapters in the United States alone. As of 2020, AA has more than two million members around the globe.

John Walsh lost his son Adam to a kidnapper and murderer in 1981. He and his wife turned their misery into a national effort to improve systems to find missing children. He helped develop the National Center for Missing and Exploited Children and launched an important TV program, *America's Most Wanted*, that aided law enforcement in their effort to capture wanted criminals.

One of the most moving stories I had the privilege to cover as a reporter was that of a concerned grandmother in Detroit who was tired of drug dealers taking over the neighborhoods in her section of the Motor City. Instead of hiding behind locked doors and barred windows, she went out to the streets and engaged members of her church community to join her. They started by organizing peaceful marches and telling the dealers to get out of Dodge. They also appealed to the city to tear down abandoned buildings, which often were centers of illegal drug activity. Within a few years, one woman, fed up with the crime that was threatening her family and her community, turned her area back into a welcoming neighborhood where children could play outside and families could have block parties, sit on their front porches, and play with their kids without fear of gunshots or other threats from thugs. Her efforts caught the attention of other residents, who did the same on their streets. All of this was started by one grandmother.

It's Not All Peaches and Cream, You Know

Are you familiar with the story of Dorothy Day? She is another profound example of someone who learned firsthand that life is neither all peaches and cream nor a bowl of cherries, and she, too, turned misery into ministry—so much so that her cause for canonization was opened in 2000 by the Archdiocese of New York and confirmed in 2012 by the United States Conference of Catholic Bishops.

Day experienced great poverty as a child. Her father, a journalist, moved the family from New York to San Francisco, where everything in their lives changed dramatically due to the earthquake of 1906. With no home or job, her father relocated the family once again, this time to Chicago. It's said that Day was so ashamed of her family's poverty that on the way home from school, she would stop in front of an impressive mansion and wave goodbye to her friends in hopes that they would think she lived there. Those experiences never left her, even after her father found work again and the family was lifted out of the Chicago slums.

Her concern for the poor led her to become an avid socialist. She worked for several socialist newspapers, trying to raise awareness about the abuses suffered by the poor, especially the immigrants at the turn of the twentieth century. While living and working in New York, she was exposed to the Catholic Faith through several Catholic women with whom she shared lodgings. They exhibited joy and a deep commitment to Christ and the Church. Day became even more attracted to Catholicism after learning of the Church's long-standing commitment to immigrants and the poor.

After her conversion in 1927, she felt that there was much to do to continue to bring a brighter spotlight on the conditions of immigrants and the poor. She eventually started the publication *The Catholic Worker* with Peter Maurin in 1933. That newspaper was the catalyst for the founding of a home for the disadvantaged. But it was more than a place where those who were hungry or without a roof over their heads could find food and shelter. Dorothy Day's House of Hospitality developed into a powerful lay movement devoted to practicing the Corporal and Spiritual Works of Mercy, modeled after the early Christians. Today the Catholic Worker Movement has grown to nearly 170 houses across America and almost 30 around the world.

An awful lot happened to this strong woman, who is now known as a Servant of God—a title given to a deceased person whose life and work are officially being investigated for possible sainthood. Day experienced the pain of an abusive relationship that led to an abortion. She even attempted suicide. She knew suffering and decided to do something about it. She remained active in the Catholic Worker Movement until her death in 1980 at the age of eighty-three.

Perhaps whatever you're going through right now won't necessarily turn into a new program impacting thousands of people. Or maybe that is exactly what the Lord has in store. In the meantime, ask God what lessons He wants you to learn right now and how the lessons you learn from your situation might help a friend, a neighbor, or someone in the pew next to you who may be going through a similar trial. I know I spent much too much time focusing on the aches and pains of the moment rather than seeking the Lord's guidance as to how that desert experience might be used for good.

In his 2007 encyclical *Spe Salvi* (*Saved in Hope*), Pope Benedict XVI reminded us that we can try to limit suffering, to fight against it, but we will not be able to eliminate it. And if we try to withdraw from what might hurt us, real joy and happiness will elude us.

It is when we attempt to avoid suffering by withdrawing from anything that might involve hurt, when we try to spare ourselves the effort and pain of pursuing truth, love, and goodness, that we drift into a life of emptiness, in which there may be almost no pain, but the dark sensation of meaninglessness and abandonment is all the greater. It is not by sidestepping or fleeing from suffering that we are healed, but rather by our capacity for accepting it, maturing through it and finding meaning through union with Christ, who suffered with infinite love. (no. 37)

Sometimes suffering is a result of our own bad choices and actions. Quite frequently, suffering is brought on by the sins of others. We don't go looking for it. As Rosie and Anna would say, it's certainly "not all peaches and cream." And yours truly can say that you would not be reading this book and I would not be where I am today in my relationship with God, my husband, and my ministry without the not-so-peachy-keen times. I would not want to go through all the messiness again. That said, those messes certainly shocked me into reality so that I could get a grip and clean up my act, so to speak.

Life's showers and thunderstorms, as Grandma pointed out, can and do rain on our parades. Anna and Rosie both taught me that the storms will pass and leave within us deeper roots.

And Anna should know because she certainly had her share of storms. She emigrated from Italy as a child in the early 1900s and married another Italian immigrant, my grandfather Pasquale, when she was a teenager. They raised ten children during the Depression years. My grandfather had challenges finding steady work because he never learned to read or write in English. He took odd jobs where he could, and when the kids were old enough, they went to work to help feed the family. My grandparents also lost a son, my uncle Donald, when he was a toddler. He was hit by a car as he ran into the street to retrieve his ball. Yet Anna and Pasquale saw a lot of flowers grow in their little corner of the East Coast. They had a strong marriage, twenty grandchildren, and even more great-grandchildren.

Is it any wonder that one of my grandmother's favorite songs, "Pennies from Heaven," contained lyrics directly connected to the peaches-and-cream saying?

> That's what storms were made for.
> And you shouldn't be afraid for.
> Every time it rains, it rains pennies from Heaven.
> Don't you know each cloud contains pennies from Heaven?
> You'll find your fortune falling all over town.
> Be sure that your umbrella is upside down.
> Trade them for a package of sunshine and flowers.
> If you want the things you love, you must have showers.
> So, when you hear it thunder, don't run under a tree.
> There'll be pennies from Heaven for you and me.

So go grab your umbrella. Turn it upside down and do your best to dance in the rain. And remember, "all sunshine makes a desert." And even though "it's not all peaches and cream," eventually that umbrella will be overflowing with more than enough joy to share.

Let Us Pray

Let Nothing Disturb You

Let nothing disturb you.
Let nothing frighten you.
All things are passing away:
God never changes.
Patience obtains all things.
Whoever has God lacks nothing;
God alone suffices. (St. Teresa of Ávila)

Reflection

Suggested Scripture Verses

All things work for good for those who love God, who are called according to his purpose. (Rom. 8:28)

In the world you will have trouble, but take courage, I have conquered the world. (John 16:33)

At dusk weeping comes for the night; but at dawn there is rejoicing. (Ps. 30:6)

Saintly Words of Wisdom

In light of heaven, the worst suffering on earth will be seen to be no more serious than one night in an inconvenient hotel. (St. Teresa of Ávila)

Our body is not made of iron. Our strength is not that of stone. Live and hope in the Lord, and let your service be according to reason. (St. Clare of Assisi)

Reflection Questions

1. In *Spe Salvi*, Pope Benedict XVI says that it's when we "attempt to avoid suffering that we drift into a life of emptiness." How often do you try to avoid suffering instead of learning from it?

----

2. What lessons do you think you might learn from a current crisis or problem?

----

3. How might you turn your "misery into ministry"?

Go Ride Your Bike

Boredom is not an option—Rosie's effort to help us appreciate life at every moment and the incredible gift of time

5

For everything there is a season, and a time
for every matter under heaven.

—Ecclesiastes 3:1, RSVCE

As a child growing up in Michigan, I couldn't wait for summer. It was and still is my favorite season of the year. Back then, I couldn't wait for the time when there was no homework and no alarm clocks to ruin my fun. I didn't have to wake up early and put on that dull, scratchy uniform. But it was much more than that. As I mentioned earlier, I love warm weather. I convinced myself that the only thing I really wanted or needed were those long, lazy, hazy days of having nothing to do but climb trees and soak up the sun. Even rainy summer days could be fun. I remember looking out the classroom window of my Catholic grade school as the year was winding down and dreaming about the afternoons ahead when I could ditch the umbrella and run in the street with the other neighborhood kids, splashing around to our hearts' content, or maybe spend hours downstairs with my dolls and other toys.

Why, then, every year after the chains of grade school were broken and summer officially was underway, would I soon be telling Rosie, "Ma, I'm bored"? Rosie would respond the same every time, with a quick and firm "Go ride your bike." She meant for me to take those words seriously. Although I didn't understand it at the time, my repeated complaints of boredom were like nails on the chalkboard to her in so many ways. I might have thought twice about complaining to my mother had I considered her upbringing—all that she never had as an East Coast inner-city kid in the thirties and forties compared with all that we had as kids growing up in the suburbs in the sixties and seventies. What was I thinking? Well, like most children, I wasn't doing much thinking, except where my own issues were concerned. Nor did I consider that as a busy mom, who had taken on a part-time job to help with the bills, she would have given anything to have a summer afternoon to do nothing at all.

My mom was raised in Jersey City during the Depression. The rugged and very industrial town of her era look nothing at all like the sparkling and sophisticated Jersey City of today—a vibrant urban center with massive skyscrapers, expensive real-estate develop-ments, beautiful boardwalks along the Hudson River, glamorous restaurants, and famous landmarks, including the Colgate Clock. How many times did I see that clock as I looked out the window of my grandma's kitchen! It was part of the old Colgate factory—the company now famous for its toothpaste, but back then, it was also a soap manufacturer. The laundry soap Octagon inspired the clock's unique shape. The Colgate factory is long gone, but the clock still stands proudly. It's popular with locals and visitors to both Jersey City and Manhattan, as it lights up brightly at night and is one of the few reminders of the city's manufacturing past. Today it is considered iconic. Back then, my mom's family considered it an eyesore and another reminder that the Upper East Side of New York City and the more pleasant neighborhoods of the Garden State, were close yet oh-so-far away.

Rosie, Angelo, Mary, Jenny, Theresa, Benny, Frankie, Elaine, and Patty didn't have stunning waterfront parks in which to frolic.

La famiglia: *Rosie with her* sorelli *and* fratelli *(sisters and brothers).*

They had the docks along the river where they would skip stones and watch the freighters and other ships pass the Statue of Liberty and Ellis Island on their way out to sea. They didn't go to the beach and build sandcastles during their summer breaks. But they were grateful when the fire department opened the fire hydrants for the neighborhood children in the heat of the summer, and they could hardly contain themselves when they were able to get to the city pool on occasion, as overcrowded as it was, with so many other city kids vying for a place to cool off.

If you were hanging out with Rosie and her brothers and sisters back then, you wouldn't see them riding bikes up and down the street or on their way to the pool or down to the Hudson docks. They didn't own bikes. None of the other kids on the block did either. They just couldn't afford what was considered an item of luxury. There were no family rooms, large bedrooms, or basements filled with board games, dolls, and other playthings.

Having grown up with so few material things, how come my mother said she was rarely bored? How was that possible with no Slinky, Hula-Hoop, go-cart, or girly-girl pink two-wheeler, such as I had growing up? When we would go back to New Jersey to visit, I loved hearing all the funny stories of my mom and her siblings as they were raised in an apartment with one bathroom and very few toys to go around. When they got tired of skipping rocks, they would jump rope or play kickball in the street. They would sit on the front stoop for hours and watch the world go by. That was the place not only to see the latest activities in the neighborhood but to be seen as well.

One of my favorite stories has to do with my mom, my aunt Theresa, the stoop, and a big dill pickle. One summer afternoon, Rosie and Theresa were enjoying their time on the stoop and chatting away. Rosie was also enjoying a big, fat, cold pickle she had just grabbed from the local market near the apartment. Suddenly she noticed that a cute boy from high school was about to pass by. She told her sister to hold the pickle while she made herself more presentable. Rosie sat up straight and gave the young man—Alfred, I think his name was—a big wave and a smile. He returned the greetings and continued down the street. When he was out of sight, she turned back to her sister to enjoy that crisp pickle. However, in the short time it took Alfred to walk by, my aunt had devoured that pickle. If that Jersey City stoop could talk, I can imagine the other interesting and funny Rosie tales it would tell.

When rain put a damper on their outdoor fun, they would huddle in their small living room and listen to my godmother, Aunt Jenny, as she made up all sorts of crazy stories to keep the brood occupied. There were even kooky contests, in which, for instance, one sister would dare the other to drink the dishwater in the sink or sneak a sip of homemade wine, just to see if they could do it without getting caught.

Despite hearing all the stories of my aunts' and uncles' exciting and endearing youthful escapades, which were filled with the simplest of activities and few, if any, shiny items from a catalogue or a local department store, I failed to connect the dots as to why they had so much fun. The "less is more" concept never crossed my mind as I stared in through the screen door on summer days, whining of boredom and watching Mom wash the floor or make dinner. Imagine what she must have been thinking as she looked back at me. She would have seen the lovely bike resting in the carport behind me. She no doubt thought about the pile of toys in the basement: countless Barbies, not to mention Little Kiddles dolls, which were also popular when I was growing up. And let's not forget the much-loved Troll dolls, which are making a big comeback today. Yes, I had them as well, along with an adorable Troll dollhouse. We were not wealthy—not by a long shot. We were a typical middle-class family, but compared with my mother and her brothers and sisters, my sisters and I had plenty of nice things to keep us occupied, including bikes—plural, not one bike between the three of us. My parents worked hard to give us what they could only dream of as kids, and I had the audacity to tell my mother I was bored. About the only thing we didn't have was a pool. More on that in the next chapter.

My parents did their best to slow down. My dad loved to make a classic Italian summer drink for him and my mom. He would cut up peaches and put them in wine, sort of an Italian version of sangria, and then they would take their wine glasses out to the patio to sip slowly and enjoy. On Sunday mornings after Mass, they would come home and enjoy a long, leisurely breakfast. They were practicing

their own version of *la dolce far niente*, the sweetness of doing nothing. Those family story hours with the relatives back in New Jersey
were also a great source of recreation and brought them such joy.

According to the experts, my folks were spot on, as making
room for down time is a must if we want to stay healthy.

"We need to give ourselves a break, and a little downtime works
well for almost everybody. It doesn't really matter what the activity or inactivity is," says emotional fitness expert and author Dr.
Barton Goldsmith.

In an article published several years ago in *Psychology Today*,
Goldsmith explained that down time is good for our mental and
physical health, as it gives our hearts and minds a chance to re-
charge and relax.

> The idea is to give your body, mind, and heart a chance to
> relax and recharge. If you keep going at full speed every day,
> it can be really hard on you, both physically and mentally.
> We were not designed to go 24/7/365 (even though that's
> become a popular modern-day mantra). It doesn't matter
> what form your idle time takes, as long as it's not destruc-
> tive. You owe yourself the gift of a deep breath and a view
> of the long sunset. And if you tell yourself that you're be-
> ing unproductive, remember that you can't function well
> if you've exhausted all your resources by never stopping to
> take a rest. Again, it doesn't matter when you do it. This is
> not about tradition. Pick whatever day and time work best
> for you, and make it a plan. By committing to take some
> time for yourself and for those you love, you are giving
> yourself and your family a gift.[16]

[16] Barton Goldsmith, PhD, "The Importance of Allowing Yourself to Relax," *Psychology Today*, November 20, 2013, https://

Studies show that boredom is what feeds creativity and imagination, something that has been slowly lost in our culture. Feeding the downtime with social media scrolling or other forms of media has hampered children's brain development, which fosters self-esteem and much-needed social skills. Dr. Jodi Musoff, MA, MEd, educational specialist from the Child Mind Institute explains:

> Boredom also helps children develop planning strategies, problem-solving skills, flexibility and organizational skills—key abilities that children whose lives are usually highly structured may lack.... It's not the boredom itself that helps children acquire these skills—it's what they *do* with the boredom. Typically, kids don't plan their days, but when they work on a project to fill their time, they have to create a plan, organize their materials and solve problems.... Developing these skills helps children better manage a variety of academic tasks, such as planning for long term assignments, and flexibility when working on group projects and social skills.

"Additionally, boredom fosters creativity, self-esteem and original thinking," the institute explains. "The key is to help kids learn how to manage their boredom so they can develop independence and feel agency over their own happiness and well-being," adds Dr. Stephanie Lee, PsyD, of the institute.[17]

Hopefully you can see by now that through her phrase "Go ride your bike," Rosie was trying to get some vital messages across.

---

www.psychologytoday.com/us/blog/emotional-fitness/201311/the-importance-allowing-yourself-relax.

[17] Gia Miller, "The Benefits of Boredom," Child Mind Institute, https://childmind.org/article/the-benefits-of-boredom/.

Everything's Coming Up Rosie

It's important to note that she also offered me the option of helping her cook and clean if I didn't stop complaining, and there were plenty of times I ended up dusting, vacuuming, or doing the laundry instead of riding that bike. Rosie wanted my sisters and me to realize that those precious seasons of summer, as well as other special periods in our lives, would not last forever. Having the ability to hop on a bike and pedal to our hearts' content was not something to take for granted. If we didn't want to ride our bikes, we should enjoy doing nothing at all. Or, as they say in Italian, *la dolce far niente*. Wasn't that what I was dreaming of just a short while back, the endless days of summer, with hours at my disposal? Sitting on that stoop doesn't sound like doing much of anything. But Rosie loved it. That's when she connected with the sights, sounds, and smells of the community. That's when she was able to soak up the rhythm of the day. It was the stuff that memories were made of—the ability to appreciate and learn more about one's surroundings.

After just one trip to Italy, *la dolce far niente* became a way of life for me and my husband. Sitting in a wine bar, having a vino or a cocktail, and just relaxing, not worrying about having another monument to check off the list: what an absolute joy. In Italy, this is a daily occurrence. Or perhaps it's the *passeggiata*, the late-afternoon or early-evening stroll in Italian cities and villages. It's not a determined walk or jog dedicated to burning off calories or achieving those ten thousand or more steps before we move to the next item on our to-do list. Instead, to Italians, it is a way to reconnect with each other and enjoy the time of day.

For busy-bee Americans, spending more than twenty minutes having a drink with friends or slowly strolling along with no real goal other than soaking in the sunset might seem like a waste of time. That's what I used to think when I was much younger. I never understood why my grandfather would spend so much time just sitting on the bench in the tiny park across the street from their apartment building. Sometimes he would feed the pigeons. Sometimes he would talk to the other old men who came by. Most of the time, he was doing nothing. But he never looked bored—just very peaceful and relaxed.

The inability to slow down, to reflect, to feed the birds, to watch the clouds go by, or to go ride your bike, for crying out loud, is a major problem in our world today. If we rode those bikes more, played more often with our children and grandchildren, or maybe worked on that model plane, think how much more balanced and less stressful life might be? Think about how often we read in Scripture of Jesus going off by Himself, or our Blessed Mother, who so often pondered things in her heart. Who ponders anymore? Do we even know what that word means? Having the luxury of time on our hands should not produce boredom, nor should we always be so worried about producing something with that time. There is, as Ecclesiastes explains, a time for everything. The time itself is what matters. So what are you waiting for? Go ride that bike.

Let Us Pray

Serenity Prayer

God, grant me the serenity
to accept the things I cannot change,
the courage to change the things I can,
and the wisdom to know the difference.

Reflection

Suggested Scripture Verses

For everything there is a season, and a time for every matter under heaven. (Eccles. 3:1, RSVCE)

Mary kept all these things, pondering them in her heart. (Luke 2:19, RSVCE)

In the morning, a great while before day, he rose and went out to a lonely place, and there he prayed. (Mark 1:35, RSVCE)

Saintly Words of Wisdom

You're bored? That's because you keep your senses awake and your soul asleep. (St. Josemaría Escrivá)

It is requisite for the relaxation of the mind that we make use, from time to time, of playful deeds and jokes. (St. Thomas Aquinas)

Those who love God will find pleasure in everything; those who do not love God will never find true pleasure in anything. (St. Alphonsus Liguori)

Reflection Questions

1. How can you embrace more *la dolce far niente*, or the art of doing nothing, in your life?

----

2. How often do you take time to reflect or ponder?

----

3. What do you do to relax, and how often do you make relaxation or downtime a part of your life?

If You Want a Pool, Go Fill Up a Gawbage Can!

As the Rolling Stones and Rosie remind us, you can't always get what you want, so make the most of what you have by seeing the glass, or the garbage can, half full instead of half empty

6

Growing up, my sisters and I were blessed to have everything we needed—and then some. We had plenty of toys, nice clothes, a small but comfortable ranch home, and always lots of good food on the table and in our lunch bags. One thing we didn't have, however, was a pool. Had you asked me how my summer was going at any point during my early childhood, I would have told you that the lack of a pool translated into what I believed was a deprived and tortured life.

A pool was something I wanted so desperately that I constantly reminded my parents of how horrible our situation was. After all, I wasn't looking for a fancy built-in pool with a diving board. All I was hoping and wishing for was a reasonably sized above-ground pool. The neighbors next door had a large above-ground oval pool. The neighbors across the street had a smaller one. Their houses were the same size as ours, so if they could afford one, why couldn't we? I promised my parents that I would take care of it. No worries about keeping it clean or adding the chlorine or whatever else was necessary; I would be the go-to cabana girl.

Everything's Coming Up Rosie

My constant nagging was apparently too much for Rosie to handle. Finally, she had heard all she was going to hear. *Basta*, or "enough," as our Italian relatives would say. She was going to put a stop to the annual start-of-summer "no pool" whining routine. My whining did not wear Rosie down—not one bit. Instead, she strongly and loudly suggested that if it was a pool we wanted, then for Heaven's sake—and these were Rosie's exact words—"go fill up a gawbage can!"

"Hmmm. Not a bad idea," I thought. On some level, I realized my mom was reacting out of sheer frustration and annoyance, but the idea of some sort of a pool was too intriguing to ignore. "If Mom and Dad won't buy us a pool, we will make our own." So off my sister and I went in search of an extra garbage can. Behind the house, we found an old one that hadn't been used in a while. We scrubbed it squeaky clean. During the creative process, our arms got sore from patting ourselves on the back, thinking we were all that and a bag of chips. It was very exciting. All the other kids had to worry about opening, closing, and cleaning their pools. Not us. We had it much easier. We filled it up with water and used a small stool to climb into our homemade contraption. By golly, we were onto something until we realized that we should have stepped into the garbage can *before* filling it up. The water in our "pool" quickly overflowed onto the driveway. So we refilled it. We then realized that when one of us got out and the other climbed in, more water would spill out.

When Rosie became aware that we had taken her words to heart, she put a stop to our "pool" use for fear that the water bill would be the eventual financial ruin of our family. Back to the sprinkler it was. Well, at least our short-lived invention kept us occupied for a little while.

Children don't understand the cost of things. They just see something on TV or at a friend's house, and they want it immediately.

If You Want a Pool, Go Fill Up a Gawbage Can!

I didn't realize that money didn't grow on trees (another popular Rosieism). My parents worked hard to send us to a good Catholic grade school. Granted, the school tuition then was a mere pittance compared with education costs today. That didn't mean it was a cakewalk for my parents, who were also trying to save up for our college education. They were good providers but were not able to give us every single thing we wanted. Not that they would have granted our every wish even if money were no object, but due to very normal expenses at the time, they had to prioritize. So a pool was not in the cards.

Our childhood years went by quickly, and we survived just fine without a pool. As silly as the statement "If you want a pool, go fill up a garbage can" may seem, it helped to get an important lesson across: that we can't always have everything we desire, material or otherwise.

Several years ago, I came upon the following poignant reflection whose author is unknown. It could even be considered food for prayer, as it's filled with some rather humbling statements and statistics regarding how blessed we are to have homes, an education, and our health. It should cause us to stop, reflect, give thanks, and pray for those less fortunate, for if we think even the most basic of things we take for granted are commonplace everywhere, as the writer points out, we need to think again.

If you have:
food in your fridge, clothes on your back, a roof over
    your head and a place to sleep ...
you are richer than 75 percent of the world.

If you have:
money in the bank, your wallet, and some spare change ...
you are among the top 8 percent of the world's wealthiest.

If you are:
attending college, or planning on attending college …
you are among the top 1 percent educated globally.

If you woke up this morning:
with more health than illness …
you are more blessed than the million people who
    will not survive this week.

If you have never experienced:
the danger of battle, the agony of imprisonment or
    torture, or the horrible pangs of starvation …
you are luckier than five hundred million people alive
    and suffering.

If you are reading this message:
you are more fortunate than three billion people
    in the world who cannot read at all.

During his July 31, 2022, Angelus message, Pope Francis stressed the spiritual need for understanding the dangers related to covetousness and greed. His reflection focused on that day's Gospel, in which Jesus shares the parable of the rich fool.

Then he told them a parable. "There was a rich man whose land produced a bountiful harvest. He asked himself, 'What shall I do, for I do not have space to store my harvest?' And he said, 'This is what I shall do: I shall tear down my barns and build larger ones. There I shall store all my grain and other goods and I shall say to myself, "Now as for you, you have so many good things stored up for many years, rest, eat, drink, be merry!"' But God said to him, 'You fool, this night your life will be demanded of you; and the things you have prepared, to whom will they belong?' Thus will it be for the one who stores up treasure for himself but is not rich in what matters to God." (Luke 12:16–21)

The pope told the pilgrims gathered in St. Peter's Square that longing to possess too much or focusing too heavily on filling up our own "barns"—as in our garages, basements, and bank accounts—can make our lives much less fulfilling and can lead to all sorts of problems, including divisions in our families and in society. In Luke's Gospel, this parable of the rich man followed the Lord's exchange with a man concerned that his brother might be cheating him out of his inheritance. Commenting on that, the pope said:

> Responding to the man, Jesus does not get into the details, but goes to the root of the divisions caused by the possession of things. He says clearly: "Take heed and beware of all covetousness" (v. 15). What is covetousness? It is the unbridled greed for possessions, always desiring to be rich. This is an illness that destroys people because the hunger for possessions creates an addiction. Above all, those who have a lot are never content, they always want more, and only for themselves. But this way, the person is no longer free: he or she is attached to, a slave of, what paradoxically was meant to serve them so [they might] live freely and serenely. Rather than being served by money, the person becomes a servant of money. But covetousness is a dangerous illness for society as well—due to covetousness, we have today reached other paradoxes: an injustice never before seen in history, where few have so much and so many have little or nothing.

In that Angelus message, Pope Francis was trying to provide Catholics and other Christians around the world with the same message Rosie was trying to impart by saying no to a pool; if we are used to always getting what we want, we will want more and will never be satisfied with what we have. Pope Francis continued:

> And so, let us try to ask ourselves: How is my detachment from possessions, from wealth, going? Do I complain about what I lack, or do I know how to be content with what I have? In the name of money or opportunity, am I tempted to sacrifice relationships and sacrifice time with others? And yet again, does it happen that I sacrifice legality and honesty on the altar of covetousness? I said "altar," the altar of covetousness, but why did I say "altar"? Because material goods, money, riches can become a cult, a true and proper idolatry. This is why Jesus warns us with strong words. He says you cannot serve two masters, and—let's be careful—he does not say God and the devil, no, or even the good and the bad, but God and wealth (cf. Lk 16:13). One would expect that he would have said that you cannot serve two masters, God and the devil. Instead, he says God and wealth. That wealth be at our service, yes; to serve wealth, no—that is idolatry, that is an offence to God.

The pope wrapped up the message by saying we need to be "rich" according to God:

> God is the richest of all. He is rich in compassion, in mercy. His wealth does not impoverish anyone, does not create quarrels and divisions. It is a richness that loves to give, to distribute, to share. Brothers and sisters, accumulating material goods is not enough to live well, for Jesus says also that life does not consist in one's possessions (cf. Lk 12:15). It depends, instead, on good relationships—with God, with

others, and even with those who have less. So, let us ask ourselves: How do I want to get rich? Do I want to get rich according to God or according to my covetousness? And, returning to the topic of inheritance, what legacy do I want to leave? Money in the bank, material things, or happy people around me, good works that are not forgotten, people that I have helped to grow and mature?

Sometimes it's hard to say no to ourselves and to our loved ones. My husband and I don't have any of our own children but are very close to our sweet grandnieces. Now I know how grandparents feel when they have that desire to shower their grandbabies with everything under the sun. It's very tempting, so my husband and I always check with my grandnieces' mom and dad to make sure we're not overdoing it. As adults, we should apply the same thought process to ourselves. Are we asking through prayer and discernment for our spiritual parents—as in God our Father and our Blessed Mother—to show us what we really need versus what we want? And how are we doing in the gratitude department?

When I think back to how deprived I felt without a pool, I must admit I'm sort of ashamed. Yes, I was only a child, but I didn't have to look very far, barely a few feet, to see all that I had. There was a large, well-maintained backyard in which to run and play to my heart's content. Rosie and her siblings didn't have a yard. They grew up in crowded apartments, with the streets as their playground. And only about two miles from our house was a beautiful public pool with diving boards and slides galore, much grander than that old and quite packed city pool in Rosie's Jersey City. Our pool in suburban Detroit was also attached to a large park that sat along a beautiful lake in our waterfront community. Not too shabby at all. And there was also that basement, my own "barn," or "silo," filled with toys. My mother told me that she and her siblings didn't get any toys at Christmas until their oldest brother, Angelo, was able to get work. Instead, for years, it was stockings filled with fruit and some candy. Those stocking stuffers, nonetheless, were enough to make them practically giddy, as sweet treats were not exactly a regular item in a Depression-era household.

I'm sure my grandparents would have desired to give their children more gifts, but the gifts they did leave them are priceless and timeless. They don't break or wear out. They are the gifts of gratitude and appreciation. Parents who've given their children everything their little hearts desire are noticing an absence of both in those children.

In 2021, the University of Michigan released a survey over the Thanksgiving holiday, at about the same time moms and dads were bombarded with those long Christmas lists from little Johnny and Susie. The researchers questioned nearly twelve hundred parents with children between the ages of four and ten. Over half admitted that they spoil their children way too much, and two in five said that it's truly embarrassing how selfishly their children act.

> "Many parents may look back to their own childhood and, in comparison, wonder if they are giving their child too much in the way of material things. Parents may have watched their child behave selfishly, such as refusing to share with other children or saying they don't like a particular gift," says the co-director of the C. S. Mott Children's Hospital National Poll, Sarah Clark.

> "We know that gratitude is associated with more positive emotions, having strong relationships, enjoying more experiences and even health benefits," she adds. "However, gratitude is not something that children usually acquire

automatically; it needs to be nurtured, in an age-appropriate way," she added.[18]

The good news is that most parents, according to this same survey, truly do want, as Clark explains, to raise appreciative children, with three out of four saying it is a high priority.

I found it very interesting that the advice from the researchers on the best ways to teach children gratitude are steps adults should also be taking:

- making "thank you" a regular phrase
- talking about gratitude
- volunteering
- giving[19]

As the Prayer of St. Francis says, "It is in giving that we receive." Perhaps it is time for us to take a closer look at what the Lord has given us and to see that the glass—or shall we say, garbage can—is half full instead of half empty.

[18] Chris Melore, "Spoiled Generation: 4 in 5 Parents Say Children Aren't Thankful for What They Have," StudyFinds, November 22, 2021, https://studyfinds.org/parents-say-children-not-thankful/.

[19] "Mott Poll: 4 in 5 Parents Say Children Today Aren't as Thankful as They Should Be," Susan B. Meister Child Health Evaluation and Research Center, November 22, 2021, https://chear.org/news-publications/2021-11-22/mott-poll-gratitude.

Let Us Pray

Prayer for Detachment

I beg of you, my Lord,
to remove anything which separates
me from you, and you from me.

Remove anything that makes me unworthy
of your sight, your control, your reprehension;
of your speech and conversation,
of your benevolence and love.
Cast from me every evil
that stands in the way of my seeing you,
hearing, tasting, savoring, and touching you;
fearing and being mindful of you;
knowing, trusting, loving, and possessing you;
being conscious of your presence
and, as far as may be, enjoying you.

This is what I ask for myself
and earnestly desire from you. Amen. (St. Peter Faber, SJ)[20]

Reflection

Suggested Scripture Verses

Whoever of you does not renounce all that he has cannot
be my disciple. (Luke 14:33, RSVCE)

---

[20] Michael Harter, SJ, ed., *Hearts of Fire: Praying with Jesuits* (Chicago: Jesuit Way, 2004), 38.

When the young man heard this he went away sorrowful; for he had great possessions. (Matt. 19:22, RSVCE)

Give thanks in all circumstances; for this is the will of God in Christ Jesus for you. (1 Thess. 5:18, RSVCE)

Saintly Words of Wisdom

The great danger for family life in the midst of any society whose idols are pleasure, comfort, and independence, lies in the fact that people close their hearts and become selfish. (Pope St. John Paul II)

Christ does not force our will, He takes only what we give Him. But He does not give Himself entirely until He sees that we yield ourselves entirely to Him. (St. Teresa of Ávila)

Remember, when you leave this earth, you can take with you nothing that you have received, only what you have given; a heart enriched by honest service, love, sacrifice, and courage. (St. Francis of Assisi)

Reflection Questions

1. What is the "swimming pool" in your life—something you've strongly desired but have not been able to achieve or receive?

2. How has this impacted your relationship with God and others?

_____
_____
_____
_____
_____

3. Are you more prone to see that glass, or garbage can, as half empty or half full?

_____
_____
_____
_____
_____

Be Nice

Rosie's recipe for following the Golden Rule

7

Do to others as you would have them do to you.

—Luke 6:31

"Be nice." That's quite a short and straightforward sentence. It's also a directive that is not followed often enough nowadays, when verbally attacking someone on social media, or in another public arena, is the standard operating procedure when there is even the slightest disagreement.

What ever happened to taking the high road and either not responding or, when we do respond, trying to engage, remaining calm and polite, and most importantly, remembering that the person on the other end of the conversation has feelings and is a child of God with great dignity, even if, in our frustration, we don't see the person that way? That, as they say, is the old fifty-thousand-dollar question. Whether in an e-mail, a tweet, a Facebook comment, or expressing ourselves in person, being nice is a lost art. The anonymity of the Internet, as well as the physical distance it provides, allows people to say to someone online what they would never have the nerve to say if that same person were standing right in front of them. And this habit enables the rudeness to spill out of us in a variety of ways and places.

The need to vent and the amount of venting going on, in my humble opinion, is out of control. My EWTN colleague and friend, psychologist and author Dr. Ray Guarendi, agrees. On my radio program, we have had many a discussion on how our culture, aided by the Internet, allows us to vent instantly while barely taking a breath to think about what we're saying or how our venting will be received. We just need to get this, that, and everything off our chests, so we will "feel better."

In one of his recent books, *Living Calm: Mastering Anger and Frustration*, Dr. Ray explains that the concept of the so-called benefits of acting on the need to blow a gasket any time we feel like it has been with us since long before advances in technology:

> Sigmund Freud long ago theorized something similar regarding matters of the mind: Anger and its companion, aggression, need to be vented; otherwise, they will reach a boiling point and wreak havoc on their vessel, the human psyche. Freud called this release catharsis.
>
> Over time this theory gained a lot of steam and diffused into the popular psyche. And why not? It seemed so obvious, so basic, so, well, scientific. In one sense it is. Medicine is emphatic: Lots of anger, particularly the ongoing, easily aroused kind, can do lots of damage—not only to one's relationships but to one's body. A host of reverberating ill effects can plague the person who doesn't find some means to settle his agitation.[21]

After years in practice, Dr. Ray concludes that even though so many "experts" in his field of psychotherapy stick to Freud's

---

[21] Dr. Ray Guarendi, *Living Calm: Mastering Anger and Frustration* (Irondale, AL: EWTN Publishing, 2022), 88.

catharsis theory, he has found that the opposite is often true. Those who vent regularly don't feel better in the long run, and they do much more harm than good, not only to themselves but to those on the receiving end of their rage.

Few people feel relieved after emotionally erupting or verbally blistering someone. Most regret what they said or did. Later they rethink what they initially thought justified, wishing for a sort of reverse catharsis. That is, they'd like to be able to retract some of the fallout. Even if venting does have possible cleansing effects, it risks exchanging one negative state for another. Consider the course of a river. It appears to meander aimlessly; it does not. Water naturally follows the path of least resistance. It will flow where its flowing is freest. Observe too how, during a rainstorm, runoff rivulets of water seem to dig their own channels. Again, they slide down the path of least resistance. And as it rains harder, they slide faster and deeper down their entrenched channels. Future storms have a ready-made path for their drenchings.

Anger follows a similar course: The more it flows, the more easily it flows, and the more quickly it flows. It's dangerous that way. A vent can become a habit can become a style can become a personality. "This is just who I am when I'm pushed too far." Still, stuffing all one's ire can't be good, can it? It will hemorrhage sometime somehow, often with little provocation. It will vent on its own. Even so, the question follows, "Does venting—willful or not—have benefits? The plain answer is no."[22]

[22] Guarendi, *Living Calm*, 89.

While psychological theories from Freud and friends, along with cell phones and laptops, are more recent developments affirming bad behavior, the bad behavior itself is part of our human condition and has been with us since the beginning of humanity. Venting with our words is just one way it is exhibited. But there are plenty of other rude actions that speak more loudly than those words.

It's not uncommon for children to forget that their parents were once young and faced many of the same issues children face today. I must admit that at times, when Rosie would encourage my sisters and me to "be nice," it would get on my nerves. I didn't think she understood how I felt about what had happened at school that day or how that bothersome neighborhood bully was at it again. She understood a lot more than I knew. Perhaps that's why this Rosieism was told to us just about every other day—or so it seemed.

Those growing up in my mom's generation had a cancel culture or rudeness of a different kind. While our modern-day cancel culture all too frequently occurs through the viciousness expressed on Twitter, Facebook, Snapchat, and numerous other popular social media outlets, the cancel culture Rosie experienced came in the form of in-person rejection based on her family's economic situation. Perhaps that is why she was so determined to see us treat others better than she had been treated.

My mother was a very attractive woman. I lost count of how many comments I heard about her beautiful smile and silky-smooth skin. Even as she grew older, those compliments continued. I heard them from people at our parish and in the grocery store; and since Mom and I had the same dentist, every time I had an appointment, the hygienist, as she was cleaning my teeth, would go on and on about lovely Rosie.

Rosie never saw herself quite that way. As feisty and strong-willed as she was, there was also in her a sense of insecurity. The little girl who had been made fun of because of her hand-me-downs was still there. That hand-me-down story was still so fresh in my mom's mind that she could share it in vivid detail years later. It happened at a school assembly. My grandmother always made sure her children were clean and their clothes nicely pressed and in order, but new outfits were hard to come by, so, like many other parents raising kids during the Depression, she was forced to send her kids off to school in clothes that had been worn quite a few times. During the assembly, my mom was placed next to one of her more well-to-do classmates. Given that there were so many poor immigrants in that part of the country during the 1930s, I'm not sure just how well off this fellow classmate was. It could be that her father was a bit more educated than my grandfather and so was able to maintain a steady job. Whatever her status, this student made a point of trying to embarrass Rosie. The girl noticed right away Mom's slightly used and most likely a bit dated frock and stared at her almost in disbelief. Rosie described it as a long look of disgust. And to make matters worse, this girl was apparently so put off by my mother's outfit that she got up and moved to another seat. My mom said that at that moment, she wanted to disappear.

When she began dating my father years later, she still didn't believe she was very pretty. On one occasion, when they were meeting other couples for dinner, my father described the scene and how proud he was, as all the eyes in the room were suddenly glued to Rosie as she entered. She thought they were looking at someone else. Why would they be looking at her? She still viewed herself as that not-good-enough, hand-me-down girl.

Fast-forward to the twenty-first century and our media-saturated world. One of the biggest concerns today is the connection between social-media usage and mental-health issues. The adage "sticks and stones may break my bones, but names will never hurt me" just doesn't ring true. Perhaps it never did. Even though it was meant to encourage us not to be bothered by the mean girls and boys who hurled insults on the playground, name-calling and insults in the classroom, on the playground, and through cyber bullying hurt a great deal. Rosie is proof of that, as are so many other people, young and old, who have experienced that our world can be anything but nice.

According to a 2021 study by the Pew Center, although young people are often the victims of cyber bullying, adults are hardly immune. In Pew's *State of Online Harassment* report, researchers found that roughly four in ten Americans experience online harassment for a variety of reasons. Among the findings, about one-fifth of those Americans who have experienced online harassment say they feel they were targeted because of their religion. Political views that aren't in conformity with "acceptable" views are also at the center of much of the bullying. We adults are no longer allowed to have our own beliefs. Unless we express the views being constantly proclaimed throughout the toxic culture, online, at town hall or school board meetings, and so on, beware. You could be the next victim.[23]

The report looked at several distinct behaviors, including these:
- offensive name-calling
- purposeful embarrassment
- stalking
- physical threats
- harassment over a sustained period of time
- sexual harassment

---

[23] Emily A. Vogels, *The State of Online Harassment*, Pew Research Center, January 13, 2021, https://www.pewresearch.org/internet/2021/01/13/the-state-of-online-harassment/.

Indeed, 20% of Americans overall—representing half of those who have been harassed online—say they have experienced online harassment because of their political views. This is a notable increase from three years ago, when 14% of all Americans said they had been targeted for this reason. Beyond politics, more also cite their gender or their racial and ethnic background as reasons why they believe they were harassed online.

While these kinds of negative encounters may occur anywhere online, social media is by far the most common venue cited for harassment—a pattern consistent across the Center's work over the years on this topic. The latest survey finds that 75% of targets of online abuse—equaling 31% of Americans overall—say their most recent experience was on social media.

Rudeness, or the failure to "be nice," is so common that I doubt if most realize just how often we might be engaging in negative behavior. It is something that is affirmed by the mass media, in movies, in music, and even in popular clichés, such as "nice guys finish last" and "the squeaky wheel gets the grease." Being nice doesn't mean being a pushover or allowing injustice. Being nice is taking the Golden Rule seriously. As Jesus told us, we need to treat other people as we want to be treated: "Do to others as you would have them do to you" (Luke 6:31). And the way we treat each other, as St. Paul stresses in Galatians, is an indication of the state of our heart and our relationship with Christ.

Now the works of the flesh are obvious: immorality, impurity, licentiousness, idolatry, sorcery, hatreds, rivalry, jealousy, outbursts of fury, acts of selfishness, dissensions, factions, occasions of envy, drinking bouts, orgies, and the like. I warn you, as I warned you before, that those who do such things will not inherit the kingdom of God.

In contrast, the fruit of the Spirit is love, joy, peace, patience, kindness, generosity, faithfulness, gentleness, self-control. Against such there is no law.

Now those who belong to Christ [Jesus] have crucified their flesh with its passions and desires. If we live in the Spirit, let us also follow the Spirit. Let us not be conceited, provoking one another, envious of one another. (Gal. 5:19-26)

Okay, so maybe you're not running around partaking in orgies, engaging in drinking bouts, or practicing sorcery. But what about that venting thing? Notice how outbursts of fury are mentioned right alongside those other serious sins? We should also take note that those outbursts can lead to other forms of sin cited by St. Paul, including dissensions, factions, and occasions of envy. And these actions are so serious they could prevent us from entering Heaven.

Let Us Pray

Prayer of St. Francis

Lord, make me an instrument of Your peace:
Where there is hatred, let me sow love.
Where there is injury, pardon,
Where there is doubt, faith,
Where there is despair, hope,
Where there is darkness, light,
and where there is sadness, joy.

Reflection

Suggested Scripture Verses

Put on then, as God's chosen ones, holy and beloved, heartfelt compassion, kindness, humility, gentleness, and patience, bearing with one another and forgiving one another, if one has a grievance against another; as the Lord has forgiven you, so must you also do. (Col. 3:12–13)

No foul language should come out of your mouths, but only such as is good for needed edification, that it may impart grace to those who hear. (Eph. 4:29)

Above all, let your love for one another be intense, because love covers a multitude of sins. Be hospitable to one another without complaining. (1 Pet. 4:8–9)

Saintly Words of Wisdom

You need to hold fast to two virtues: kindness toward your neighbors and humility toward God. (St. Padre Pio)

Be the living expression of God's kindness: kindness in your face, kindness in your eyes, and kindness in your smile. (St. Teresa of Calcutta)

One who plants kindness gathers love. (St. Basil)

Reflection Questions

1. How have you seen unkindness exhibited recently in your circle of family or friends?

_____

_____

_____

_____

2. How did you respond?

_____

_____

_____

_____

3. Do you need to ask forgiveness for a recent act of unkindness?

_____

_____

_____

_____

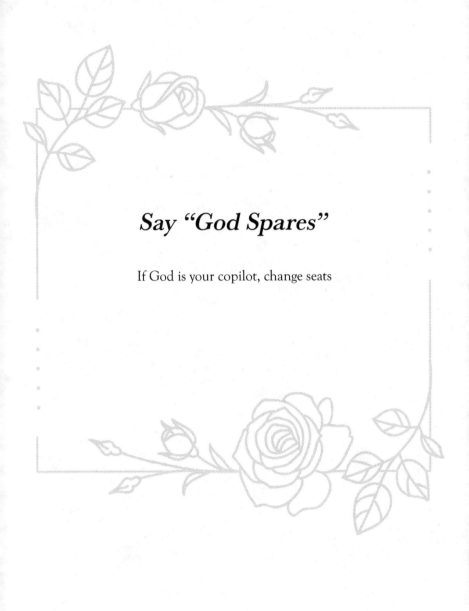

Say "God Spares"

If God is your copilot, change seats

8

Come now, you who say, "Today or tomorrow we shall go into such and such a town, spend a year there doing business, and make a profit"—you have no idea what your life will be like tomorrow. You are a puff of smoke that appears briefly and then disappears. Instead you should say, "If the Lord wills it, we shall live to do this or that."

—James 4:13-15

"Ma, what in the world are you saying?" I finally blurted out that question after hearing Rosie say, for the millionth time, "God spares." With her heavy eastern accent, it sounded more like "God spayuz." Even when she said the phrase slowly, it was hard to understand. When I eventually figured out the words, I was still puzzled by their meaning. Rosie seemed to express those words automatically whenever we were about to do something or go somewhere. When, for example, my sisters and I were getting excited about going on another one of our family adventures to visit relatives in New Jersey, Ma would always pipe up. She wouldn't let us get too far into the daydreaming or the vacation talk without her usual "God spares." It was her way of reminding us of who was in charge, and it was not us. It wasn't as if she didn't want us to look forward to the good times; she just always wanted us to remember that everything is in God's providence. St. Thomas

Aquinas teaches us about the amazing attributes of God—that God is omniscient (all knowing), omnipotent (all powerful), and omnipresent (everywhere, at all times, no matter what). But have I ever pondered that to the full?

I must admit that many times as a young person I found the phrase annoying. "Okay, Ma, we get it," I would say. But I really didn't. At least not until years later, after giving it much prayer and reflection. Looking back on my parents' life, it made perfect sense. Imagine surviving something as dramatic as an apartment explosion and then packing up your family to move halfway across the country, leaving everything and everyone you know and love behind. Back when we were growing up, therapy or counseling after a tragedy wasn't very common. Only the rich could afford to speak with someone other than a priest or a close friend about their struggles. My parents, like most people in their era, just did their best to plow through with the help of their faith and their extended family.

In addition to losing our home, and before our parents decided it was time for a change, we had to move in temporarily with my grandparents in their Jersey City flat. For my sisters and me, it was a treat. We loved our grandparents dearly and enjoyed spending time with two of our favorite aunts who lived with them: Theresa and Mary. They were and still are so elegant, even in their nineties. They were also very warm and a great deal of fun. Our grandfather would always treat us to Wise potato chips and cream soda at night when we gathered around the one TV in their house to watch a program or a game show. I absolutely loved walking down the street to the Hudson River waterfront with my grandpa and sitting on the stoop, watching all the people go by. I still am a city girl at heart. While my grandmother was cooking, I would often sit in a window seat in the kitchen and watch her closely. Perhaps that's where I got the cooking bug, as cooking is one of my favorite pastimes, especially preparing Italian dishes.

We children felt as if we were on an extended summer holiday. My parents, not so much. They were busy trying to reclaim our belongings from what was left of the apartment building as well as trying to figure out where we were going to live. They were also trying to process what had happened. They would later tell me it was a mixture of shock and intense gratitude. After all, as I mentioned, two people died because of that blast, and others were hurt. It must have been extremely difficult trying to keep a smile on their faces for us while dealing with the trauma. We were all alive and healthy, thanks be to God. But then there was the realization that they were starting over.

If all of that weren't enough to deal with, there was the infamous oven incident with my mother. It was a Friday afternoon, and she wanted to give my grandmother a break from the cooking, so she decided to make everyone a delicious baked-fish dinner. I was in the kitchen when the accident happened. Rosie had gone through a great deal of trouble. She went to the market, made wonderful side dishes, and set Grandma's large oval kitchen table beautifully. She was hoping the special meal would help get my dad's mind off the many issues they were facing. I remember my mother opening the oven and a mixture of smoke and flames suddenly bursting forth, singeing my mother's eyebrows and burning both of her arms. The injuries to her arms required medical attention. When my father arrived back at the apartment, I ran down the stoop steps and tried to tell him that Mommy got burned, but he couldn't quite take it in. It was just too much.

That's when we were given another treat. When Dad saw my mother's arms wrapped in bandages and what must have been a pathetic look of weariness on her face, he packed us all up. The next thing we knew, we were in the car headed for the Jersey Shore. The saltwater did wonders for Rosie's burns. But most importantly, the ocean breezes and the change of scenery—far away from the city and the explosion—were just what the doctor ordered for both Mom and Dad. My sisters and I were giddy with delight, playing on the beach, and having a blast in the hotel pool. As a matter of fact, one of my favorite pictures is one of me in my father's arms as we were swimming in that pool. It sits on the end table in my living room. Looking at that picture, one would never know what had recently transpired. We both look so happy.

Not long after the summer of the explosion, my father received a call from his older brother, who had moved his family to Michigan. My uncle Steve, an electrical engineer, was hired by a small but growing engineering firm in Detroit, and the firm was looking for a mechanical engineer. My parents thought this was a real sign that God wanted them to start over in the Great Lakes State. The cost of living was much lower in the Midwest, and there were good and affordable opportunities for my parents to own a home rather than rent—something that most likely was not going to happen if they stayed on the East Coast. So off we went.

When you're a child, you can bounce back from difficulties, depending on how your parents react. My sisters and I didn't realize how tough things were, as my parents made it seem like another family escapade. No wonder Rosie said "God spares" so frequently.

Years later, when I was doing a women's Bible study, I came across these verses in the New Testament Letter of St. James:

> Come now, you who say, "Today or tomorrow we shall go into such and such a town, spend a year there doing business, and make a profit"—you have no idea what your life will be like tomorrow. You are a puff of smoke that appears

briefly and then disappears. Instead you should say, "If the Lord wills it, we shall live to do this or that." (4:13–15)

I almost fell out of my chair. "If the Lord wills it"! I kept staring at those words. "That's Rosie!" I said out loud to myself and quickly picked up the phone to tell my mother just how very biblical she was. She thought it was amazing that her saying was scriptural. I think that's when her words really sank in.

The importance of recognizing God as Lord of our lives is prominent throughout Scripture. These verses do not imply that we should live chaotic lives without any planning or scheduling. We just need to be always aware that everything is a gift and that not a single breath is taken without the grace or the will of God.

Take, for example, the parable of the rich man's harvest in Luke 12:

There was a rich man whose land produced a bountiful harvest. He asked himself, "What shall I do, for I do not have space to store my harvest?" And he said, "This is what I shall do: I shall tear down my barns and build larger ones. There I shall store all my grain and other goods and I shall say to myself, 'Now as for you, you have so many good things stored up for many years, rest, eat, drink, be merry!'" But God said to him, "You fool, this night your life will be demanded of you; and the things you have prepared, to whom will they belong?" Thus will it be for the one who stores up treasure for himself but is not rich in what matters to God. (vv. 16–21)

My husband, Deacon Dominick, gave a great homily based on this Gospel message, which is reflected by St. James in his letter. When I heard my husband preach, I smiled as a thought of the wisdom of my Rosie Posie again.

The Gospel parable might be a little puzzling at first because it almost seems God is going to take the man's life because he has been successful and prosperous. It's not that God doesn't want these things for us, but He does want us to put Him first in our lives. In one of the psalms, it says: Do not put your hope in riches even when they increase. God wants us to put Him first in our lives because He knows that our ultimate fulfillment as persons resides in Him.

So why, then, does God call the man in the parable a fool? The first thing we notice is how the man consults only himself about how to respond to his prosperity—saying several times, "I will do this" and "I will do that," et cetera. Six times he uses the word *I*, and not once does he mention or thank God. Secondly, if we look at the root of the word that is translated "myself," we find it refers to a person's life or soul. So this passage could be read as the man saying: "I will pull down my barns and build larger ones; and there I will store all my grain and my goods. And I will say to my soul: soul you have ample goods laid up for many years; take your ease, eat, drink, and be merry." ...

In reading the parable this way, we can see that the rich man believes he is the master of his own soul; that's why he is a fool. Only God has reign over our souls, our lives, and everything else we have in this world; and I'm not just talking about material possessions.

Whether you say "God spares" or "God willing"—words that, by the way, are now a regular part of my vocabulary—repeating that phrase as you go about your activities will help you keep things in the proper perspective.

Let Us Pray

In the Hands of God (I Was Born for You)[24]

I am Yours and born of You;
What do You want of me?
Majestic Sovereign,
Unending wisdom,
Kindness pleasing to my soul;
God sublime, one Being Good,
Behold this one so vile.
Singing of her love to You:
What do You want of me?
Yours, You made me,
Yours, You saved me,
Yours, You endured me,
Yours, You called me,
Yours, You awaited me,
Yours, I did not stray.
What do You want of me?
Good Lord, what do You want of me,
What is this wretch to do?
What work is this,
This sinful slave, to do?
Look at me, Sweet Love,
Sweet Love, look at me,
What do You want of me?
In Your hand I place my heart,

[24] Vuestra soy, para vos nací.

Body, life, and soul,
Deep feelings and affections mine,
Spouse—Redeemer sweet,
Myself offered now to You,
What do You want of me?
Give me death, give me life,
Health or sickness,
Honor or shame,
War or swelling peace,
Weakness or full strength.

Yes, to these I say,
What do You want of me? . . .

Yours I am, for You I was born:
What do You want of me?
(St. Teresa of Ávila)

Reflection

Suggested Scripture Verses

Come now, you who say, "Today or tomorrow we shall
go into such and such a town, spend a year there doing
business, and make a profit"—you have no idea what your
life will be like tomorrow. You are a puff of smoke that
appears briefly and then disappears. Instead you should
say, "If the Lord wills it, we shall live to do this or that."
(James 4:13–15)

But God said to him, "Fool! This night your soul is required of you; and the things you have prepared, whose will they be?" (Luke 12:20)

Not everyone who says to me, "Lord, Lord," will enter the kingdom of heaven, but only the one who does the will of my Father in heaven. (Matt. 7:21)

Saintly Words of Wisdom

Do not fear what may happen tomorrow. The same loving Father who cares for you today will care for you tomorrow and every day. Either He will shield you from suffering, or He will give you unfailing strength to bear it. Be at peace, then, and put aside all anxious thoughts and imaginings. (St. Francis de Sales)

Lay all your cares about the future trustingly in God's hands and let yourself be guided by the Lord just like a little child. (St. Teresa Benedicta of the Cross)

The secret of happiness is to live moment by moment and to thank God for all that He, in His goodness, sends to us day after day. (St. Gianna Molla)

Reflection Questions

1. Are you more like Rosie or the rich man in Luke's Gospel?

   _____

   _____

   _____

   _____

2. In addition to saying "God spares" or "God willing," what other similar holy habits could you develop to grow closer to Christ and His Church?

   _____

   _____

   _____

   _____

3. Do you put God first in everything in your life, or do you seek His guidance only in major concerns or events?

   _____

   _____

   _____

   _____

Nevva Get Too Big for Those Britches

Inflated egos can and will be easily deflated

9

Whoever exalts himself will be humbled; but
whoever humbles himself will be exalted.

—Matthew 23:12

"Please don't recognize me." I kept saying this to myself as I waited in a very long line at the unemployment office in suburban Detroit less than a week after I was fired from my TV news job. In those days, the early 1990s, almost everything related to receiving unemployment compensation had to be done in person. Talk about the exalted being humbled! Wasn't it just the other night that my face was plastered all over the TV, reporting the latest on a major story of national significance? And yet there I was with people from all walks of life and all different positions, all in the same boat, waiting to file an unemployment claim.

The waiting seemed like hours, thanks mainly to the busybody who was standing in the line across from me and just staring. Maybe he thought I reminded him of a relative or a long-lost girlfriend or classmate. That's what I was sincerely hoping. Surely, he didn't recognize me. How quickly things change! One minute, I loved being in the limelight and having people point me out at the mall, the grocery store, or the hair salon. But now I just wanted to run and hide.

"Hey, aren't you Teresa Tomeo?" he practically shouted across the room. "Didn't I just see you on Channel 50 the other night, doing the news?" Suddenly his eyes weren't the only ones staring directly at me. Thank goodness the Lord gave me lots of experience that enabled me to think quickly on my feet.

"Funny you should say that," I replied. "People tell me all the time that I look like her."

I wasn't sure if he bought it, but it did shut him up, and the rest of the folks just chuckled and returned to chatting with one another or reading their newspapers as we all waited our turn.

As I continued to stand in line, grateful that I at least quelled the curiosity, I couldn't help but hear Rosie's voice: "Nevva get too big for those britches." In the years of success and notoriety I had been experiencing, I had forgotten her wise warning. The word *ego* became an acronym that described the way I lived. I had, quite frankly, "eased God out" of everything, thinking I didn't need Him. My career had been going swimmingly. Okay, my marriage was at the breaking point, and my faith life was nonexistent, but hey, I will get to those relationships later, I would tell myself. I put God, my husband, close friends, and family on the back burner all for the sake of my career, looking out for only me, myself, and I. That's what was drilled into me in journalism school and by the radical feminist culture that was developing in the seventies and the eighties. Women were expected to put themselves and their careers ahead of everyone and everything else if they wanted to be success-ful. Little did I know it could all be taken away from me so quickly.

The saying "Nevva get too big for those britches," although another Rosie favorite, was not a Rosie original. Hardly. It dates way back before her time—apparently, all the way back to good ol' Davy Crockett, best known from the 1950s TV shows about his life, in which he was referred to as "king of the wild frontier."

Crockett was a United States congressman who represented the state of Tennessee in the nineteenth century. The britches cliché was first found in an 1835 publication written by the politician and colonel himself and titled *An Account of Colonel Crockett's Tour to the North and Down East*: "I myself was one of the first to fire a gun under Andrew Jackson. I helped to give him all his glory. But I liked him well once: but when a man gets too big for his breeches, I say Goodbye."

The saying became popular in the South along with a version with the variation "too big for their boots." It is basically used to describe someone who acts as if he or she is better or more important than others. And I quite frankly had become an expert at doing just that. I really thought I was untouchable. Who was I kidding?

My parents were very proud of me and my accomplishments as a broadcast journalist, and they enjoyed watching me on the evening news and listening to me on the radio. But they were the first, with Rosie taking the lead as I was growing up, to knock me down a few pegs when I needed it. Living through the lean years of the Depression as children and then being knocked way out of their comfort zone and out of the comfortable life they had built in Jersey City by that horrific gas explosion, they had learned the hard way that none of us should think too much of ourselves or our circumstances. Those teaching moments continued into my adult years as my career began to soar, but I didn't really pay attention—at least not until I was fired. More than once, Rosie would tell me, "You may be on television, but rememba, I'm still your mutha."

If you think that having a major faith reawakening would wipe out the EGO, or "easing God out," factor in my life, think again. St. Paul reminds us in Romans that we all sin and all fall short of the glory of God (3:23). If we're still here, God is not through with us yet. And oh, how St. Paul's words, and Rosie's, rang loud and clear back in 2007, when I received an invitation to attend a Vatican women's congress in Rome.

I'll never forget the day when I went to the mailbox and saw a package with my name on it along with the Vatican seal. I quickly opened the envelope and read the letter, and apparently, I read it too quickly. I could not contain my excitement over what those pages contained. So I ran to the phone to call my husband, but I forgot that he was in class that night at the seminary. Next on the list to call was my spiritual director. He wasn't available either. And then I called my good friend, well-known Catholic evangelist and teacher Fr. John Riccardo. He didn't answer, but I had to tell someone close to me, or I would explode, so I left him a message, bragging about the letter and my very important assignment.

"Padre, it's T. Guess who wants me to present at a women's meeting in Rome next year—the Vatican! Isn't that fantastic? Call me ASAP."

As I went to grab the letter to read more about what I thought would be my amazing moment in the Roman sun, I wondered what I would address in my presentation, where I would be staying, and how I might be able to get Catholic radio to cover my big Vatican debut. The conference was months away, and I was already there, front and center, sitting next to a cardinal, a bishop—hey, maybe even Pope Benedict! So much for "God willing" or "God spares." Those visions of grandeur, however, suddenly disappeared when I took more time to read what was written, as opposed to what I thought was written.

We would like you to be present at the Vatican congress for women, commemorating the twentieth anniversary of John Paul II's letter *On the Dignity and Vocation of Women* (*Mulieris Dignitatem*).

Now considering that a relatively small number of women from different countries around the world were invited to serve as delegates, or to "be present," it was still quite a blessing and an honor. And it indeed was an experience I will never forget. But there is, of course, a major difference between *being present* and *presenting*.

As I was eating that big piece of humble pie, I decided it would be a good idea to call Fr. John and leave another message.

"Uh, hi, Padre, it's T again. Well, they don't want me to present, but they do want me to *be present* as this event. Call me when you can." I felt like such a jerk.

Fr. John called me back a short time later, but I couldn't understand him. He had listened to both messages and was laughing so hard it sounded as if he were hyperventilating. One more lesson to add to that faith notebook.

The *Modern Catholic Dictionary* describes *humility* as, among other things, "the virtue that restrains the unruly desire for personal greatness and leads people to an orderly love of themselves." This orderly love is

> based on a true appreciation of their position with respect to God and their neighbors. Religious humility recognizes one's total dependence on God; moral humility recognizes one's creaturely equality with others. Yet humility is not only opposed to pride; it is also opposed to immoderate self-objection which would fail to recognize God's gifts and use them according to His will.

So we need to be humble enough to recognize the gifts given to us by our Creator and confident enough in God's will for our lives to follow through by using those gifts to make a difference.

St. Teresa of Ávila's poem "In the Hands of God" (see the prayer at the end of the previous chapter) is more like a very long, deep prayer recognizing that we were made in the image and likeness of God, created by Him for a specific purpose. Throughout the poem, this great mystic—the first female to be named a Doctor of the Church—keeps asking the same question we should all be asking the Lord daily, if we truly want to be His humble servants.

"I am Yours and born of You; what do You want of me?" Notice how this question, prevalent throughout this saint's prayer, is very similar to our Blessed Mother's fiat at the Annunciation, after St. Gabriel announces to her that she has been chosen to be the Mother of God.

"Mary said, 'Behold, I am the handmaid of the Lord. May it be done to me according to your word.' Then the angel departed from her" (Luke 1:38).

The *Catechism of the Catholic Church* says humility is such an important part of our faith life that it is considered the foundation of prayer—not *a* foundation or one of many building blocks but *the* foundation of prayer.

> "Prayer is the raising of one's mind and heart to God or the requesting of good things from God." But when we pray, do we speak from the height of our pride and will, or "out of the depths" (Ps. 130:1) of a humble and contrite heart? He who humbles himself will be exalted (cf. Luke 18:9-14); *humility* is the foundation of prayer. Only when we humbly acknowledge that "we do not know how to pray as we ought" (Rom. 8:26), are we ready to receive freely the gift of prayer. "Man is a beggar before God."[25]

---

[25] *Catechism of the Catholic Church* (CCC) 2559, quoting St. John Damascene, *De fide orth.* 3, 24: *PG* 94, 1089C; St. Augustine, *Sermo* 56, 6, 9: *PL* 38, 381.

How many times have I approached God in prayer without humility, failing to remember to whom I am speaking and spending my prayer time telling Him, the Alpha and the Omega, the Beginning and the End, the Creator of the universe, what He needed to do for me? Here was my plan, and for me, it was the desire, after I came back to the Church and landed back in the secular media in a big way, to stay in the news business. And if He would only put His rubber stamp on *my* plan, we could be besties. I treated God and faith as a slot machine and waited for the big win. I put in the coins, so to speak, such as saying some prayers and going to Mass, asking for this, that, or the other thing that I was so certain would make me happy. I pulled the one-armed bandit, and when I didn't get my way, or win a prize, I chose to view God as a mean ogre in the sky trying to squash my happiness. I should instead have seen Him as a loving parent who knows what's best for me.

Now I realize that God had a much bigger and better plan for me than I could ever have imagined and that involved using my media gifts differently. After a long tug-of-war with God, when I had another "offering it up" or surrender moment, God slowly began revealing a different but much more spiritually prosperous path that continues to give me real joy and happiness in ways I never expected or could have imagined.

If you're a parent, how often have you said no to your child because you saw the reality or the result of granting your child's desires. Your child may not have understood at the time but later realized that your no was actually a yes. Your child's wish could have been something as simple as having more snacks before bed or staying up later on a school night. Giving in to those seemingly small requests could not only lead to short-term issues but could also encourage long-term unhealthy habits. You're looking at the big picture, and so is God.

Obviously, I still had and have more to learn about not getting too big for those britches or boots. The Vatican letter was hardly my last humility challenge. But no worries there, as Rosie, even toward the end of her life, was still capable of helping me remain humble.

Rosie adored my husband. Dominick reminded her of my dad—kind and gentle. My husband is an engineer like my dad, and he treated my mother so well. He had such patience with her and was always there to step in when the stress of her elder care was taking its toll not only on me but on my relationship with my mother. I joked with friends and family that Rosie loved Dom more than she loved her own daughter. I often thought that when I visited her at her assisted-living facility. I would race over to see her after my radio show, sometimes several times a week. She wasn't exactly around the corner, and when I would walk into her apartment, often frustrated after fighting traffic and construction, she would look at me, smile, and then look around me, expecting Dominick to be there, even though it was the middle of the day, and he was at work. Before even saying hello, she would ask, "Where's your husband?" Another moment to practice humility.

For years, Rosie was part of an interdenominational prayer group, which she really enjoyed. She would often ask me questions about a particular Scripture verse or another faith-related topic. At first, I thought she valued my input. Given that, by that time, I had a few books and years of Catholic radio experience under my belt, I assumed she would be satisfied with my explanations. I soon came to realize that it was more of her simply enjoying a conversation. She didn't really want my advice or reflections. She was very outgoing and loved to talk and was eager, even in her old age, to learn more about God and the Catholic Faith.

She would listen politely, but nine times out of ten, the conversation would end with something like "That's very interesting.

When does your husband get home?" It was Dominick who was the deacon. He was the one with the theology degree and the vestments. I was just her daughter. Another slice of humble pie, anyone?

Well, I'm certainly not alone when it comes to struggling with the difficulty of being humble. Our social-media-saturated world has helped to aid and abet an already self-centered society. If we just take the selfie category, the statistics will make your head spin. The latest research from 2021 and 2022, for example, shows that:

- Ninety-two million selfies are taken every day.
- Individuals spend fifty-four hours a year, or seven minutes a day, taking selfies.
- Millennials will take 25,700 selfies in their lifetime.
- More than half of plastic surgeons report increases in patients wanting procedures to make them look better in selfies. In 2016, those requests jumped 13 percent.[26]

And that's just one of many studies on our obsession with self and selfies. Even if we're not self or selfie obsessed, we know, as Christians, that we all have a long way to go when it comes to emulating the humility of Christ, our Blessed Mother, and our Catholic saints. But that's okay, as long as we keep trying.

Now that Rosie's gone, I'm still getting plenty of opportunities to practice humility, and I don't have to go very far. My adorable grandnieces, identical twins Francesca and Lilliana, are all too happy to make sure that Aunt Tree Tree (their nickname for me) doesn't get too big for her britches. Even though the twins live close to us in southeastern Michigan, I just can't get enough of seeing them. Dominick and I connect with them through Facetime as often as possible to check in and see how their day is going and

---

[26] Broz, "28 Selfie Statistics."

to look at their sweet faces. And it never fails: within a matter of a New York minute, one or both of the twins will begin channeling their great-grandmother by asking, "Aunt Tree Tree, can we talk to Uncle Dommie?" Would you like some whip cream on that second piece of humble pie?

Rosie—and her uncanny ability to knock me off my high horse occasionally—lives on through her great-granddaughters. And thank goodness—because the Lord knows I still need it. How about you?

Let Us Pray

Litany of Humility

O Jesus! meek and humble of heart, *hear me.*

From the desire of being esteemed, *deliver me, Jesus.*
From the desire of being loved ...
From the desire of being extolled ...
From the desire of being honored ...
From the desire of being praised ...
From the desire of being preferred to others ...
From the desire of being consulted ...
From the desire of being approved ...
From the fear of being humiliated ...
From the fear of being despised ...
From the fear of suffering rebukes ...
From the fear of being calumniated ...
From the fear of being forgotten ...
From the fear of being ridiculed ...
From the fear of being wronged ...
From the fear of being suspected ...

That others may be loved more than I,
Jesus, grant me the grace to desire it.
That others may be esteemed more than I ...
That, in the opinion of the world, others may increase
    and I may decrease ...
That others may be chosen and I set aside ...
That others may be praised and I unnoticed ...

That others may be preferred to me in everything . . .
That others may become holier than I, provided that
    I may become as holy as I should . . .

Reflection

Suggested Scripture Verses

Likewise, you younger members, be subject to the presbyters. And all of you, clothe yourselves with humility in your dealings with one another, for: "God opposes the proud but bestows favor on the humble." So, humble yourselves under the mighty hand of God, that he may exalt you in due time. (1 Pet. 5:5–6)

The result of humility and fear of the LORD is riches, honor, and life. (Prov. 22:4)

Put on then, as God's chosen ones, holy and beloved, heartfelt compassion, kindness, humility, gentleness, and patience, bearing with one another and forgiving one another, if one has a grievance against another; as the Lord has forgiven you, so must you also do. (Col. 3:12–13)

Saintly Words of Wisdom

He who wants to learn true humility should reflect upon the Passion of Jesus. (St. Faustina)

There is more value in a little study of humility and in a single act of it than in all the knowledge in the world. (St. Teresa of Ávila)

Reflection Questions

1. Was there a time in your life when you might have been "too big for those britches"?

   _____

   _____

   _____

   _____

   _____

2. Who or what helped you to recognize the need for more humility?

   _____

   _____

   _____

   _____

   _____

3. Do you take the time to reflect on the incredible humility of Christ, God incarnate?

   _____

   _____

   _____

   _____

   _____

Keep Smiling

Learning to embrace true JOY: Jesus first, others second, yourself last, regardless of life's circumstances

10

Do not be saddened this day, for rejoicing
in the LORD is your strength!"

—Nehemiah 8:10

Our journey of faith doesn't have to be complicated. And that really is one of the main reasons I decided to write down Rosie's top-ten list — to help us live a godly life. Her lessons are very simple, direct, and yes, sometimes very funny, but oh-so-applicable to everyday life. And hopefully, you've been able to see in the pages of this book that they are also backed up by Scripture, Catholic teaching, the natural law, and a good amount of secular research. But wait, there's more, as those infomercials often proclaim: these Rosieisms are even worthy of being in papal documents.

For example, our final item on the top-ten list is mom's suggestion to keep smiling. She didn't just say this verbally. Mom would sign every single card she sent or gave someone — and it didn't matter who it was or what the occasion: birthday, anniversary, Christmas, Easter — with those same words. My dad would concur with her by using the Italian word for "mushroom": no *fungo* faces, or no sour faces.

The importance of being a joyful witness of our Faith is so important that Pope Francis dedicated an apostolic exhortation to the subject: *The Joy of the Gospel*. To emphasize the point concerning the need for joy, he drew from the insights of another pope, St. John XXIII, who also told the faithful to be concerned about an attitude of doom and gloom:

> Fifty years after the Second Vatican Council, while distressed by the troubles of our age and far from naive optimism, our greater realism must not mean any less trust in the Spirit or less generosity. In this sense, we can once again listen to the words of Blessed John XXIII on the memorable day of 11 October 1962: "At times we have to listen, much to our regret, to the voices of people who, though burning with zeal, lack a sense of discretion and measure. In this modern age they can see nothing but prevarication and ruin.... We feel that we must disagree with those prophets of doom who are always forecasting disaster, as though the end of the world were at hand. In our times, divine Providence is leading us to a new order of human relations which, by human effort and even beyond all expectations, are directed to the fulfillment of God's superior and inscrutable designs, in which everything, even human setbacks, leads to the greater good of the Church."[27]

Building on the sage advice from Pope John XXIII, Pope Francis goes even further, stating that it is very dangerous to our psyches and, more importantly, to our souls, to turn a smile into a frown and constantly wear that fungo or mushroom face.

[27] Pope Francis, apostolic exhortation *Evangelii Gaudium* (November 24, 2013), no. 84, quoting St. John XXIII, Address for the Opening of the Second Vatican Council (11 October 1962): 4, 2-4: AAS 54 (1962), 789.

One of the more serious temptations which stifles boldness and zeal is a defeatism which turns us into querulous and disillusioned pessimists, "sourpusses."

Who would ever have guessed that a description or term as common as *sourpuss* would be used in something as official as an important teaching document from the Vicar of Christ? "Go figya," as Rosie would say.

Just for the fun of it, I did a Google search to find out how many times this approach to life is referenced in the Bible. The word *joy* is used more than 150 times in Scripture, 100 times in the Old Testament and 51 times in the New Testament, so it must be a big deal in the eyes of God. As with so many of Rosie's other top-ten items, I heard or read these two words (keep smiling) from her for most of my life. So what was she trying to teach me?

Given the level of sorrow and suffering in our present age, some might see this phrase as naïve or Pollyannaish. "Everything is wonderful. No worries. Let's just tiptoe through those rows and rows of tulips and not worry about a thing." Whether it was during my mom's era, the era of the baby boomers, or the current generation, so many popular songs reminded us to whistle a happy tune or to keep doing that happy dance. In the 1950 film *Summer Stock*, Judy Garland belted out "Get Happy." When I was growing up, the theme song for the extremely popular ABC sitcom *The Partridge Family*, was "C'mon, Get Happy." More recently, Pharrell Williams had everyone at the 2014 Academy Awards—not to mention the rest of us—snapping our fingers and dancing in the aisles, anywhere and everywhere else, to his catchy number, with that same theme: "Happy."

Fun tunes help us lighten our load, at least temporarily. We can't help but put a smile on our faces, not to mention a little spring in our step, when we hear that kind of uplifting music. That's great, but that wasn't the only kind of happiness that Rosie was referring to when she told us to "keep smiling." And the same goes for God and His Church. It's a combination or a balance of enjoying our everyday existence—again to quote Pope Francis—while keeping our eyes on the prize: our reunion in Heaven with Jesus.

> This is the joy which we experience daily, amid the little things of life, as a response to the loving invitation of God our Father: "My child, treat yourself well, according to your means.... Do not deprive yourself of the day's enjoyment" (Sir 14:11, 14). What tender paternal love echoes in these words!
>
> The Gospel, radiant with the glory of Christ's cross, constantly invites us to rejoice. A few examples will suffice. "Rejoice!" is the angel's greeting to Mary (Lk 1:28). Mary's visit to Elizabeth makes John leap for joy in his mother's womb (cf. Lk 1:41). In her song of praise, Mary proclaims: "My spirit rejoices in God my Savior" (Lk 1:47). When Jesus begins his ministry, John cries out: "For this reason, my joy has been fulfilled" (Jn 3:29). Jesus himself "rejoiced in the Holy Spirit" (Lk 10:21). His message brings us joy: "I have said these things to you, so that my joy may be in you, and that your joy may be complete."[28]

In John's Gospel, we read about Jesus' first miracle, at the Wedding Feast at Cana. Having had the privilege of visiting the Holy Land on more than a dozen pilgrimages, I learned that weddings in our Lord's time—and it is still the custom today—would last not just for hours but for days. The music, the food, the fellowship, and

---

[28] Pope Francis, *Evangelii Gaudium*, nos. 4–5.

the wine, of course, kept flowing. Therefore, it would be downright silly if we thought that Jesus never stepped out on the dance floor with His mother to help celebrate that wedding two thousand plus years ago. Or that He wasn't laughing around the reception table as the families broke bread together. Although Scripture does not reference these realities specifically, we have learned through history, archaeology, and oral tradition how to look at the Bible in its full context. God was enjoying His creation at that wedding feast, and we should do the same.

I mentioned that people always commented on my mother's beautiful smile and her beautiful skin. Perhaps one of the reasons her skin was so radiant, even as she aged, was that she practiced what she preached and kept smiling through it all.

I came across several studies that show a correlation between smiling and not only our outward appearance but our inner levels of peace and joy. It takes fewer muscles to smile than it does to frown, so more smiling and fewer wrinkles. Another study shows that smiling can serve as a sort of antidepressant. Other research shows that smiling can help you live longer, and here's why.

In a study titled *Happy People Live Longer: Subjective Well-Being Contributes to Health and Well-Being*, released in 2011, researchers from the International Association of Applied Psychology found that maintaining a positive mood may be an important part of a healthy lifestyle.

> Stress can permeate our entire being, including showing up in your face and expression. Smiling not only helps to prevent us from looking tired, worn down, and overwhelmed, but it can actually help decrease stress. Believe it or not, smiling can reduce stress, even if you don't feel like smiling or even if you fake it with a smile that isn't genuine. When

you are stressed, try intentionally putting a smile on your face. It may help improve your mood and ability to manage the stress you are experiencing.

The physical act of smiling activates pathways in your brain that influence your emotional state—meaning that by adopting a happy facial expression, you can "trick" your mind into entering a state of happiness. This effect works whether or not your smile is genuine. A simple smile can trigger the release of neuropeptides that improve your neural communication. It also causes the release of neurotransmitters, such as dopamine and serotonin, which can boost your mood. Think of smiling as a natural antidepressant.[29]

And if you want to be a light of the world, as Jesus told us in Matthew 5:14, then, by all means, keep smiling, as those same researchers say it's contagious.

Your brain automatically notices and interprets other people's facial expressions—and sometimes, you may even mimic them. That means you might spot someone else's smile and unconsciously smile yourself.

Think about how tense it can be when you have a Debbie Downer in the room. I'm not referring to someone who struggles with clinical depression or is going through a difficult time. I'm talking about the type of person—and we all know one—who has nothing good to say about anything or anyone. Just as smiling is contagious, a bad attitude or mood can have the same effect. It's like a cold or flu. This is not to say that we should ignore the many

---

[29] Mark Stibich, PhD, "10 Big Benefits of Smiling," Verywell Mind, updated September 10, 2022, https://www.verywellmind.com/top-reasons-to-smile-every-day-2223755.

needs of the world as well as the many problems that exist in the Church. It does mean we need to be aware of issues and be willing to address them while being joyful disciples.

> The joy of the Gospel is such that it cannot be taken away from us by anyone or anything (cf. Jn 16:22). The evils of our world — and those of the Church — must not be excuses for diminishing our commitment and our fervor. Let us look upon them as challenges which can help us to grow. With the eyes of faith, we can see the light which the Holy Spirit always radiates in the midst of darkness, never forgetting that "where sin increased, grace has abounded all the more" (Rom 5:20). Our faith is challenged to discern how wine can come from water and how wheat can grow in the midst of weeds.[30]

If you're going through a tough time right now, it might be difficult to keep smiling. Even if you're not experiencing great suffering on a personal level, it can often be a struggle to remain joyful, or to see the glass as half full versus half empty, when there is so much pain, division, and confusion swirling around us.

As Pope Benedict XVI told the faithful in an Angelus message during Advent of 2007, despite the problems of our fallen world, it still is possible to "rejoice in the Lord always" (Phil. 4:4), if we truly believe that God is with us. This message was given on the third Sunday of Advent, known as Gaudete Sunday. *Gaudete* is the Latin word for "rejoice."

> Christian joy thus springs from this certainty: God is close, he is with me, he is with us, in joy and in sorrow, in sickness

[30] Pope Francis, *Evangelii Gaudium*, no. 84.

and in health, as a friend and faithful spouse. And this joy endures, even in trials, in suffering itself. It does not remain only on the surface; it dwells in the depths of the person who entrusts himself to God and trusts in him.[31]

If we continue to read Scripture and study our Catholic Faith, we will be able to apply what Rosie meant by her signature message, "keep smiling." I've already detailed some of the suffering my mother endured in her life, so what was it that motivated her to keep handing on that advice? I believe her life's experience helped her achieve a healthy balance. Let's take another look at that top-ten list.

1. Awfa it up to God, and put it at the foot of the Crawse.
2. Rememba, the Blessed Mutha is watching you.
3. Listen to your mutha.
4. It's not all peaches and cream, you know.
5. Go ride your bike.
6. You want a pool, go fill up a gawbage can!
7. Be nice.
8. Say "God spares."
9. Nevva get too big for those britches.
10. Keep smiling.

Notice how the points on that list are all interconnected. *Offering it up to God* and saying *"God spares,"* for example, help us stay focused on God and make good use of our sufferings. We bring our struggles and our sorrows to the Cross, and we know that everything begins and ends with Christ. Realizing that *it's not all peaches and cream* encourages in us an attitude of gratitude and

---

[31] Pope Benedict, Angelus, December 16, 2007.

leads to the ability to *smile*, in good times and in bad. Being told to go *fill up a garbage can* and *ride your bike* enables us to remember how blessed we are to live in such a prosperous country, despite all its many current challenges. Remembering that the *Blessed Mother is watching us* is an encouragement to live virtuously and appreciate the role of the Blessed Mother in our lives and in the life of the Church. *Listening to our mother* helps us respect authority in Heaven and on earth. *Being nice* and *not getting too big for those britches* helps us apply the Golden Rule.

Although Rosie and I did not always see eye to eye, I know she did her best to pass on the beliefs and guidelines that helped her live a godly and joyful life. And even though she has been gone from this earth for some time, she continues to help me in this pilgrimage called life. I hope Rosie Posie and her top-ten list can do the same for you.

Let Us Pray

Prayer to St. Philip Neri

O holy St. Philip Neri, patron saint of joy, you who trusted Scripture's promise that the Lord is always at hand and that we need not have anxiety about anything, in your compassion, heal our worries and sorrows and lift the burdens from our hearts. We come to you, whose heart swelled with abundant love for God and all creation. Hear us, we pray, especially in this need (make your request here). Keep us safe through your loving intercession, and may the joy of the Holy Spirit, which filled your heart, St. Philip, transform our lives and bring us peace. Amen.

Reflection

Suggested Scripture Verses

Do not be saddened this day, for rejoicing in the LORD is your strength! (Neh. 8:10)

Rejoice in the Lord always. I shall say it again: rejoice! (Phil. 4:4)

Although you have not seen him you love him; even though you do not see him now yet believe in him, you rejoice with an indescribable and glorious joy, as you attain the goal of [your] faith, the salvation of your souls. (1 Pet. 1:8–9)

Saintly Words of Wisdom

What peace can we hope to find elsewhere if we have none within us? (St. Teresa of Ávila)

Spiritual joy is as necessary to the soul as blood is to the body. (St. Francis of Assisi)

May God protect me from gloomy saints. (St. Teresa of Ávila)

Reflection Questions

1. How much time do you spend focusing on the negative or being a "sourpuss"?

----

2. What steps can you take to embrace more joy in your life, regardless of your circumstances?

3. Were you aware of the powerful impact smiling can have on your physical and mental health?

_____
_____
_____
_____
_____

Resources

Spiritual Resources for Self-Reflection

Theological Virtues

Faith is the theological virtue by which we believe in God and believe all that he has said and revealed to us, and that Holy Church proposes for our belief, because he is truth itself. By faith "man freely commits his entire self to God" (*DV* 5). For this reason the believer seeks to know and do God's will. (CCC 1814)

Hope is the theological virtue by which we desire the kingdom of heaven and eternal life as our happiness, placing our trust in Christ's promises and relying not on our own strength, but on the help of the grace of the Holy Spirit. (CCC 1817)

Charity is the theological virtue by which we love God above all things for his own sake, and our neighbor as ourselves for the love of God. (CCC 1822)

Cardinal Virtues

Prudence is the virtue that disposes practical reason to discern our true good in every circumstance and to choose the right means of achieving it; "the prudent man looks where he is going" (Prov. 14:15). "Keep sane and sober for your prayers" (1 Pet. 4:7). Prudence is "right reason in action," writes St. Thomas Aquinas, following Aristotle (St. Thomas Aquinas, *STh* II–II, 47, 2). It is not to be confused with timidity or fear, nor with duplicity or dissimulation. It is called *auriga virtutum* (the charioteer of the virtues); it guides the other virtues by setting rule and measure. It is prudence that immediately guides the judgment of conscience. The prudent man determines and directs his conduct in accordance with this judgment. With the help of this virtue we apply moral principles to particular cases without error and overcome doubts about the good to achieve and the evil to avoid. (CCC 1806)

Justice is the moral virtue that consists in the constant and firm will to give their due to God and neighbor. Justice toward God is called the "virtue of religion." Justice toward men disposes one to respect the rights of each and to establish in human relationships the harmony that promotes equity with regard to persons and to the common good. The just man, often mentioned in the Sacred Scriptures, is distinguished by habitual right thinking and the uprightness of his conduct toward his neighbor. (CCC 1807)

Fortitude is the moral virtue that ensures firmness in difficulties and constancy in the pursuit of the good. It strengthens the resolve to resist temptations and to overcome obstacles in the moral life. The virtue of fortitude enables one to conquer fear, even fear of death, and to face trials and persecutions. It disposes one even to renounce and sacrifice his life in defense of a just cause. (CCC 1808)

Temperance is the moral virtue that moderates the attraction of pleasures and provides balance in the use of created goods. It ensures the will's mastery over instincts and keeps desires within the limits of what is honorable. The temperate person directs the sensitive appetites toward what is good and maintains a healthy discretion: "Do not follow your inclination and strength, walking according to the desires of your heart" (Sir. 5:2; cf. Sir. 37:27-31). (CCC 1809)

The Ten Commandments

Learn about the Ten Commandments at http://IfULoveMe.org.

1. I, the Lord, am your God. You shall not have other gods besides me.
2. You shall not take the name of the Lord, your God, in vain.
3. Remember to keep holy the Lord's day.
4. Honor your father and your mother.
5. You shall not kill.
6. You shall not commit adultery.
7. You shall not steal.
8. You shall not bear false witness against your neighbor.
9. You shall not covet your neighbor's wife.
10. You shall not covet your neighbor's goods.

Sin

There are a great many kinds of sins. Scripture provides several lists of them. The *Letter to the Galatians* contrasts the works of the flesh with the fruit of the Spirit: "Now the works of the flesh are plain: fornication, impurity, licentiousness, idolatry, sorcery, enmity, strife, jealousy, anger, selfishness, dissension, factions, envy, drunkenness, carousing, and the like. I warn you, as I warned you before, that those who do such things shall not inherit the Kingdom of God" (Gal. 5:19-21; cf. Rom. 1:28-32; 1 Cor. 6:9-10; Eph. 5:3-5; Col. 3:5-9; 1 Tim. 1:9-10; 2 Tim. 3:2-5).

Sins can be distinguished according to their objects, as can every human act; or according to the virtues they oppose, by excess or defect; or according to the commandments they violate. They can also be classed according to whether they concern God, neighbor, or oneself; they can be divided into spiritual and carnal sins, or again as sins in thought, word, deed, or omission. The root of sin is in the heart of man, in his free will, according to the teaching of the Lord: "For out of the heart come evil thoughts, murder, adultery, fornication, theft, false witness, slander. These are what defile a man" (Matt. 15:19-20). But in the heart also resides charity, the source of the good and pure works, which sin wounds. (CCC 1852-1853)

Capital Sins

Vices can be classified according to the virtues they oppose, or also be linked to the *capital sins* which Christian experience has distinguished, following St. John Cassian and St. Gregory the Great. They are called "capital" because they engender other sins, other vices. They are: pride, avarice [or greed], envy, wrath [or anger], lust, gluttony, and sloth or acedia [or apathy]. (CCC 1866)

The Beatitudes

The Beatitudes are at the heart of Jesus' preaching. They take up the promises made to the chosen people since Abraham. The Beatitudes fulfill the promises by ordering them no longer merely to the possession of a territory, but to the Kingdom of heaven:
- Blessed are the poor in spirit, for theirs is the kingdom of heaven.
- Blessed are those who mourn, for they shall be comforted.
- Blessed are the meek, for they shall inherit the earth.

- Blessed are those who hunger and thirst for righteousness, for they shall be satisfied.
- Blessed are the merciful, for they shall obtain mercy.
- Blessed are the pure in heart, for they shall see God.
- Blessed are the peacemakers, for they shall be called sons of God.
- Blessed are those who are persecuted for righteousness' sake, for theirs is the kingdom of heaven.
- Blessed are you when men revile you and persecute you and utter all kinds of evil against you falsely on my account. Rejoice and be glad, for your reward is great in heaven. (Matt. 5:3–12; CCC 1716)

Corporal Works of Mercy

- Feed the hungry.
- Give drink to the thirsty.
- Clothe the naked.
- Shelter the homeless.
- Visit the sick.
- Visit the imprisoned.
- Bury the dead.

Spiritual Works of Mercy

- Counsel the doubtful.
- Instruct the ignorant.
- Admonish the sinner.
- Comfort the afflicted.
- Forgive all offenses.
- Bear wrongs patiently.
- Pray for the living and the dead.

Gifts of The Holy Spirit

Wisdom   Fortitude
Understanding   Knowledge
Counsel   Piety
Fear of the Lord

Fruits of the Holy Spirit

Charity   Generosity
Joy   Gentleness
Peace   Faithfulness
Patience   Modesty
Kindness   Self-control
Goodness   Chastity

Prayers and Devotions

Morning Offering

O Jesus, through the Immaculate Heart of Mary, I offer You my prayers, works, joys, and sufferings of this day for all the intentions of Your Sacred Heart, in union with the Holy Sacrifice of the Mass throughout the world, for the salvation of souls, the reparation of sins, the reunion of all Christians, and in particular for the intentions of the Holy Father this month. Amen.

The Lord's Prayer

Our Father, who art in Heaven, hallowed by Thy name; Thy kingdom come; Thy will be done on earth as it is in Heaven. Give us this day our daily bread; and forgive us our trespasses as we forgive those who trespass against us; and lead us not into temptation, but deliver us from evil. Amen.

Resources

Hail Mary

Hail Mary, full of grace. The Lord is with thee. Blessed art thou among women, and blessed is the fruit of thy womb, Jesus. Holy Mary, Mother of God, pray for us sinners, now and at the hour of our death. Amen.

Glory Be

Glory be to the Father, and to the Son, and to the Holy Spirit. As it was in the beginning, is now, and ever shall be, world without end. Amen.

Apostles' Creed

I believe in God, the Father Almighty, Creator of Heaven and earth; and in Jesus Christ, His only Son Our Lord, who was conceived by the Holy Spirit, born of the Virgin Mary, suffered under Pontius Pilate, was crucified, died, and was buried. He descended into Hell; the third day He rose again from the dead; He ascended into Heaven, and is seated at the right hand of God, the Father Almighty; from thence He shall come to judge the living and the dead. I believe in the Holy Spirit, the holy Catholic Church, the communion of saints, the forgiveness of sins, the resurrection of the body and life everlasting. Amen.

The Holy Rosary

Consider offering one decade of the Rosary daily. It is a powerful way to grow in your faith. See "How to Pray the Rosary," EWTN, https://www.ewtn.com/catholicism/devotions/how-to-pray-13648.

Fátima Decade Prayer

O my Jesus, forgive us our sins, save us from the fires of Hell. Lead all souls to Heaven, especially those most in need of Thy mercy.

Fátima Pardon Prayer

My God, I believe, I adore, I hope, and I love You! I beg pardon for those who do not believe, do not adore, do not hope, and do not love You. (Repeat three times.)

Guardian Angel Prayer

Angel of God, my guardian dear, to whom God's love commits me here, ever this day be at my side, to light and guard, to rule and guide. Amen.

St. Michael Prayer

St. Michael the Archangel, defend us in battle; be our defense against the wickedness and snares of the devil. May God rebuke him, we humbly pray; and do thou, O Prince of the heavenly host, by the power of God, thrust into Hell Satan and all the other evil spirits who prowl about the world seeking the ruin of souls. Amen.

Angelus

V. The angel of the Lord declared unto Mary;
R. And she conceived by the Holy Spirit.
Hail, Mary ...

V. Behold the handmaid of the Lord.
R. Be it done unto me according to your word.
Hail, Mary ...

V. And the Word was made flesh,
R. And dwelt among us.
Hail, Mary ...

V. Pray for us, O holy Mother of God,
R. That we may be made worthy of the promises of Christ.

Let us pray: Pour forth, we beseech You, O Lord, Your grace into our hearts, that we, to whom the incarnation of Christ, Your Son, was made known by the message of an angel, may by His Passion and Cross be brought to the glory of His Resurrection, through the same Christ our Lord. R. Amen.

Consecration to Mary

O Mary, Virgin most powerful and Mother of mercy, Queen of Heaven and Refuge of sinners, we consecrate ourselves to thine Immaculate Heart. We consecrate to thee our very being and our whole life; all that we have, all that we love, all that we are. To thee we give our bodies, our hearts, and our souls; to thee we give our homes, our families, our country.

We desire that all that is in us and around us may belong to thee and may share in the benefits of thy motherly benediction. And that this act of consecration may be truly efficacious and lasting, we renew this day at thy feet the promises of our Baptism and our first Holy Communion.

We pledge ourselves to profess courageously and at all times the truths of our holy Faith and to live as befits Catholics who are duly submissive to all the directions of the pope and the bishops in communion with him.

We pledge ourselves to keep the commandments of God and His Church, in particular to keep holy the Lord's Day.

We likewise pledge ourselves to make the consoling practices of the Christian religion, and above all, Holy Communion, an integral part of our lives, insofar as we shall be able so to do.

Finally, we promise thee, O glorious Mother of God and loving Mother of men, to devote ourselves wholeheartedly to the service of thy blessed devotion, in order to hasten and ensure, through the sovereignty of thine Immaculate Heart, the coming of the Kingdom of the Sacred Heart of thine adorable Son, in our own hearts and in those of all men, in our country and in all the world, as in Heaven, so on earth. Amen.

Magnificat

My soul proclaims the greatness of the Lord,
my spirit rejoices in God my Savior,
for He has looked with favor on His lowly servant.
From this day all generations will call me blessed:
the Almighty has done great things for me,
and holy is His Name.

He has mercy on those who fear Him
in every generation.
He has shown the strength of His arm;
He has scattered the proud in their conceit.

He has cast down the mighty from their thrones
and has lifted up the lowly.
He has filled the hungry with good things,
and the rich He has sent away empty.

He has come to the help of His servant Israel,
for He remembered His promise of mercy,
the promise He made to our fathers,
to Abraham and his children forever.

Evening Examination of Conscience

What sins have I committed today in thought, word, deed, and omission against God, my neighbor, and myself?

Resources

Act of Contrition

My God, I am sorry for my sins with all my heart. In choosing to do wrong and failing to do good, I have sinned against You, whom I should love above all things. I firmly intend, with Your help, to do penance, to sin no more, and to avoid whatever leads me to sin. Our Savior Jesus Christ suffered and died for us. In His name, my God, have mercy.

Prayer of Trust

My Lord God, I have no idea where I am going. I do not see the road ahead of me. I cannot know where it will end. Nor do I really know myself, and the fact that I think that I am following Your will does not mean that I am actually doing so. But I believe that the desire to please You does, in fact, please You. And I hope I have that desire in all I am doing. I hope that I will never do anything apart from that desire. And I know that if I do this, You will lead me by the right road, though I may seem to be lost in the shadow of death. I will not fear, for You are ever with me, and You will never leave me to face my perils alone.

Divine Mercy
- "How to Pray the Chaplet," The Divine Mercy, https://www.thedivinemercy.org/message/devotions/chaplet.
- "Jesus, I trust in You!" "The Divine Mercy Message and Devotion," The Divine Mercy, https://www.thedivinemercy.org/message.

Act of Consecration to the Sacred Heart of Jesus

I give myself and consecrate to the Sacred Heart of our Lord Jesus Christ my person and my life, my actions, pains, and sufferings, so that I may be unwilling to make use of any part of my being other than to honor, love, and glorify the Sacred Heart. This is my unchanging purpose—namely, to be all His and to do all things for the love of Him, at the same time renouncing with all my heart whatever is displeasing to Him. I therefore take You, O Sacred heart, to be the only object of my love, the guardian of my life, my assurance of salvation, the remedy of my weakness and inconstancy, the atonement for all the faults of my life, and my sure refuge at the hour of death.

Be then, O Heart of goodness, my justification before God the Father, and turn away from me the strokes of His righteous anger. O Heart of love, I put all my confidence in You, for I fear everything from my own wickedness and frailty, but I hope for all things from Your goodness and bounty.

Remove from me all that can displease You or resist Your holy will; let your pure love imprint Your image so deeply upon my heart, that I shall never be able to forget You or to be separated from You.

May I obtain from all Your loving kindness the grace of having my name written in Your Heart, for in You I desire to place all my happiness and glory, living and dying in bondage to You. Amen.

Litany of St. Joseph

Lord, have mercy on us. *Lord, have mercy on us.*
Christ, have mercy on us. *Christ, have mercy on us.*
Lord, have mercy on us. *Lord, have mercy on us.*
Christ, hear us. *Christ, graciously hear us.*

God the Father of Heaven, *have mercy on us.*
God the Son, Redeemer of the World . . .
God the Holy Spirit . . .
Holy Trinity, one God . . .

Holy Mary, *pray for us.*
St. Joseph ...
Renowned offspring of David ...
Light of Patriarchs ...
Spouse of the Mother of God ...
Guardian of the Redeemer ...
Chaste guardian of the Virgin ...
Foster father of the Son of God ...
Diligent protector of Christ ...
Servant of Christ ...
Minister of salvation ...
Head of the Holy Family ...
Joseph most just ...
Joseph most chaste ...
Joseph most prudent ...
Joseph most strong ...
Joseph most obedient ...
Joseph most faithful ...
Mirror of patience ...
Lover of poverty ...
Model of workers ...
Glory of family life ...
Guardian of virgins ...
Pillar of families ...
Support in difficulties ...
Solace of the wretched ...
Hope of the sick ...
Patron of exiles ...
Patron of the afflicted ...
Patron of the poor ...

Patron of the dying …
Terror of demons …
Protector of Holy Church …

Lamb of God, who takes away the sins of the world,
spare us, O Jesus.
Lamb of God, who takes away the sins of the world,
graciously hear us, O Jesus.
Lamb of God, who takes away the sins of the world,
have mercy on us, O Jesus.
He made him the lord of his household
and prince over all his possessions.
Let us pray:

O God, in Your ineffable providence, You were pleased to choose Blessed Joseph to be the spouse of Your most holy Mother; grant, we beg You, that we may be worthy to have him for our intercessor in Heaven whom on earth we venerate as our protector: You who live and reign forever and ever.

Saint Joseph, *pray for us.*

Resources to Help You Grow in Knowledge, Faith, and Holiness

Catholic News Outlets

Catholic News Agency: https://www.catholicnewsagency.com/
National Catholic Register: https://www.ncregister.com/
EWTN News: https://www.ewtnnews.com/
EWTN News Nightly: https://www.ewtn.com/tv/shows
/ewtn-news-nightly
EWTN News In Depth: https://www.ewtn.com/tv/shows
/ewtn-news-in-depth
Vatican News: https://www.vaticannews.va/en.html

Resources

Aleteia: https://aleteia.org/
New Advent: https://www.newadvent.org/
Catholic World Report: https://www.catholicworldreport.com/
Our Sunday Visitor: https://www.osvnews.com/
The Pillar: https://www.pillarcatholic.com/

Catholic Radio Programs

Catholic Connection with Teresa Tomeo: https://avemariaradio
.net/program/catholic-connection/
Kresta in the Afternoon: https://avemariaradio.net/program
/kresta-in-the-afternoon/
Epiphany: https://avemariaradio.net/program/epiphany/
Son Rise Morning Show: https://www.ewtn.com/radio/shows
/son-rise-morning-show
Women of Grace: https://www.ewtn.com/radio/shows
/women-of-grace-radio
The Doctor Is In: https://avemariaradio.net/program
/the-doctor-is-in/
EWTN radio shows: https://www.ewtn.com/radio/shows
Christ Is the Answer: https://avemariaradio.net/program
/christ-is-the-answer/
The Catholic Current: https://thestationofthecross.com
/programs/the-catholic-current/

Catholic Broadcast Media

Ave Maria Radio: https://avemariaradio.net/
Eternal Word Television Network (EWTN): https://www
.ewtn.com/
Relevant Radio: https://relevantradio.com/
Vatican Radio: http://www.radiovaticana.va/

Catholic Periodicals

OSV Newsweekly: https://www.osvcatholicbookstore.com
/Newsstand/our-sunday-visitor

L'Osservatore Romano: https://www.osvcatholicbookstore.com
/newsstand/losservatoreromano

OSV Kids: https://www.osvcatholicbookstore.com/newsstand
/osvkids

National Catholic Register: http://www.ncregister.com/

Marian Helper: https://marian.org/marian-helper-magazine

The Deacon: https://www.osvcatholicbookstore.com/newsstand
/deacondigest

First Things: https://www.firstthings.com/current-edition

Popular Catholic Websites

EWTN: https://www.ewtn.com/

Catholic Answers: https://www.catholic.com/

Discerning Hearts: https://www.discerninghearts.com/

Catholic News & Inspiration (Patti Maguire Armstrong):
http://www.pattimaguirearmstrong.com/

Susan Tassone (the Purgatory Lady): https://susantassone.com/

MassTimes.org (find a Mass near you): https://masstimes.org/

The Coming Home Network: https://chnetwork.org/

Epic Pew: https://epicpew.com/

Catholic Exchange: https://catholicexchange.com/

Integrated Catholic Life: https://integratedcatholiclife.org/

Daily Devotionals

Magnificat: https://www.magnificat.net/

The Word Among Us: https://wau.org/

One Bread, One Body: https://www.presentationministries
.com/#daily-mass-reflections

Resources

Examination of Conscience

Daily examination of conscience: https://www.ewtn.com
/catholicism/library/examination-of-conscience-12577

Ignatian Spirituality's Daily Examen: https://www.ignatian
spirituality.com/ignatian-prayer/the-examen

Examination of Conscience before Penance: https://www.ewtn
.com/catholicism/library/sacrament-of-penance-examination
-of-conscience-9121

Bible Studies and Group Studies

Catholic Scripture Study International: https://tanbooks.com
/catholic-programs/catholic-scripture-studies-css/

A Bible Study Guide for Catholics series by Fr. Mitch
Pacwa, SJ: https://www.osvcatholicbookstore.com/
Search?q=fr+mitch+pacwa

The Bible in a Year with Fr. Mike Schmitz: https://ascension
press.com/pages/biy-registration

Great Adventure Catholic Bible Study: https://ascensionpress
.com/pages/the-great-adventure

Dr. Scott Hahn's free online Bible studies: https://stpaulcenter
.com/bible-studies/text-studies/

God's Recipe for a Wonderful Life (Ten Commandments):
https://ifuloveme.org/

EWTN Scripture & Tradition with Fr. Mitch Pacwa, SJ:
https://www.ewtn.com/tv/shows/scripture-and-tradition
-with-fr-mitch-pacwa

Resources for Men

Be a Man! by Father Larry Richards: https://www.thereason
forourhope.org/shop/

Knights of Columbus: https://www.kofc.org/en/

National Men's Leadership Alliance: https://www.catholic
   menleaders.org/
Dads.org (Steve Wood): https://dads.org/
Those Catholic Men: https://thosecatholicmen.com/
The Catholic Gentleman: https://catholicgentleman.com/
That Man Is You (TMIY): https://paradisusdei.org/that
   -man-is-you/
Integrity Starts Here (helping men break free from porn addic-
tion): https://www.peterkleponis.com/
Courage (for those with same-sex attraction): https://couragerc
   .org/

Resources for Women

EWTN's *The Catholic View for Women*: http://www.thecatholic
   viewforwomen.com/
WINE—Women in the New Evangelization: https://catholic
   vineyard.com/
Women of Grace (Johnnette Benkovic Williams): https://www
   .womenofgrace.com/
CatholicMom.com: https://www.catholicmom.com/
Catholic Mom's Café (Donna-Marie Cooper O'Boyle): https://
   www.donnacooperoboyle.com/blog/
Blessed Is She: https://blessedisshe.net/
Walking with Purpose Bible study: https://walkingwith
   purpose.com/
Catholic Women's Forum: https://catholicwomensforum.org/
Letter to Women by Pope St. John Paul II: https://www.vatican
   .va/content/john-paul-ii/en/letters/1995/documents/hf
   _jp-ii_let_29061995_women.html
Mulieris Dignitatem (*The Dignity and Vocation of Women*) by Pope
   St. John Paul II: https://www.vatican.va/content/john-paul-ii

/en/apost_letters/1988/documents/hf_jp-ii_apl
_19880815_mulieris-dignitatem.html

Redemptoris Mater (*Mother of the Redeemer*) by Pope St. John
Paul II: https://www.vatican.va/content/john-paul-ii/
en/encyclicals/documents/hf_jp-ii_enc_25031987
_redemptoris-mater.html

Benedicta Institute for Women: https://www.womenofgrace.
com/benedicta

ENDOW (Educating on the Nature and Dignity of Women):
https://www.endowgroups.org/

Courage (for those with same-sex attraction): https://couragerc
.org/

Resources on Marriage

The Alexander House (Julie and Greg Alexander): https://www
.thealexanderhouse.org/

Institute for Marital Healing (Dr. Richard Fitzgibbons): https://
www.maritalhealing.com/

Marriage Encounter: https://wwme.org/

Retrouvaille (for troubled Catholic Marriages): https://
retrouvaille.org/

Beloved (Augustine Institute): https://www.augustineinstitute
.org/program-categories/marriage-beloved

*Intimate Graces: How Practicing the Works of Mercy Brings Out
the Best in Marriage* (Teresa Tomeo and Deacon Dominick
Pastore): https://teresatomeo.com/books/

Restoring Trust (for couples struggling with porn in their
marriage): https://www.peterkleponis.com/

Teresa Tomeo's marriage page: https://teresatomeo.com
/marriage/

Resources for Teens and Young Adults

EWTN's *Life on the Rock*: https://www.ewtn.com/tv/shows
/life-on-the-rock

FOCUS — Fellowship of Catholic University Students: https://
www.focus.org/

Young Catholic Professionals: https://www.youngcatholic
professionals.org

Theology on Tap: https://renewtot.org/en/

Life Teen: https://lifeteen.com/

Net Ministries: https://netusa.org/

Steubenville Youth and Young Adult Conferences: https://
steubenvilleconferences.com/

Young Women of Grace: https://www.womenofgrace.com
/study-programs#cat16

The Culture Project: https://restoreculture.theculture
project.org/

Creatio: https://creatio.org/

Resources for Parents and Families

Dr. Meg Meeker: https://www.meekerparenting.com/

More2Life with Dr. Greg and Lisa Popcak: https://avemaria
radio.net/program/more-2-life/

Intentional Catholic Parenting: https://intentionalcatholic
parenting.com/

Ascension Kids: https://ascensionpress.com/pages/kids

Teaching Catholic Kids: https://teachingcatholickids.com/

Catholic Familyland: https://msf-america.org/blog/103
-catholic-family-land

Loyola Press Family Resources: https://www.loyolapress.com
/catholic-resources/family/

Resources

Big Hearted Families and *Amazing Grace for Families* (Patti Maguire Armstrong): http://www.pattimaguirearmstrong.com/p/books.html

Sunday Gospel Activities (CatholicMom.com): https://www.catholicmom.com/sunday-mass-activities

Evangelization Programs and Ministries

ChristLife Catholic Ministry for Evangelization: https://christlife.org/

FORMED (Augustine Institute): https://formed.org/

Real Life Catholic (Chris Stefanick): https://reallifecatholic.com/

Unleash the Gospel (Archdiocese of Detroit): https://www.unleashthegospel.org/

The Coming Home Network (*The Journey Home*): https://chnetwork.org/

New Leaven: http://www.newleaven.org/

Crossroads Initiative (Dr. Marcellino D'Ambrosio): https://www.crossroadsinitiative.com/

Catholic Retreats/Centers/Conferences

Cursillo: https://www.natl-cursillo.org/

Malvern Retreat House: https://www.malvernretreat.com/

Life in the Spirit Seminar/Catholic Charismatic Renewal diocesan websites: https://www.nsc-chariscenter.org/about-us/other-ccr-groups/archdiocesan-renewal-websites/

Online Spiritual Exercises with Fr. Ed Broom, OMV (English and Spanish): https://www.youtube.com/user/FrEdBroomomv

Marian Servants of Divine Providence retreats: https://divineprovidence.org/

Jesus Thirsts for America: https://www.spiritfilledevents.com
/about-i-thirst

Marians of the Immaculate Conception retreats and events:
https://marian.org/event-list

Continuing Catholic Education

Avila Institute: https://avila-institute.org/

Augustine Institute: https://www.augustineinstitute.org/

Lighthouse Catholic Media (Augustine Institute): https://
www.lighthousecatholicmedia.org/

Lifelong Learning (Saint Benedict Press/Tan Books): https://
tanbooks.com/lifelong-learning/

Symbolon (Augustine Institute): https://www.lighthouse
catholicmedia.org/symbolon

Word on Fire (Bishop Robert Barron): https://www.wordon
fire.org/

St. Paul Center for Biblical Theology (Dr. Scott Hahn): https://
stpaulcenter.com/

Catholic Spiritual Direction (Dan Burke): https://spiritual
direction.com/

Pro-Life Resources

March for Life: https://marchforlife.org/

Priests for Life: https://www.priestsforlife.org/

LifeNews: https://www.lifenews.com/

Silent No More Awareness Campaign: https://silentnomore
awareness.org/Index.aspx

Rachel's Vineyard (abortion healing): https://www.rachels
vineyard.org/

USCCB pro-life activities: https://www.usccb.org/prolife

Resources

Teresa Tomeo list of pro-life resources: https://teresatomeo.com
/resources/

Pro-life media training with Teresa Tomeo: https://teresatomeo
.com/speaking/

Catholic Pilgrimages

T's Italy: Traveling to Italy with Teresa Tomeo in Your Pocket:
https://www.travelitalyexpert.com/

Pilgrimages to EWTN and the Shrine of the Most Blessed
Sacrament at the Our Lady of the Angels Monastery: https://
www.ewtn.com/pilgrimage

Corporate Travel Services: https://www.ctscentral.net/

Footprints of God Pilgrimages with Steve and Janet Ray:
https://www.footprintsofgodpilgrimages.com/

Catholic Podcasts

Discerning Hearts: https://www.discerninghearts.com/

Word on Fire Show (Bishop Robert Barron): https://www.word
onfire.org/videos/wordonfire-show/

Catholic Answers Live: https://www.catholic.com/audio

The Reason for Our Hope (Father Larry Richards): https://
player.fm/series/series-2359982

Doctor, Doctor podcasts (Catholic Medical Association): https://
doctordoctor.org/

American Catholic History Podcast: https://americancatholic
history.org/

EWTN podcasts (*Open Line, Miracle Hunter, Father Spitzer's
Universe, Bookmark,* and many others): https://www.ewtn.com
/radio/podcasts

Catholic Apps

Laudate: https://apps.apple.com/us/app/laudate-1-catholic
-app/id499428207

Pray as You Go (daily guided meditation): https://pray-as
-you-go.org/

EWTN: https://www.ewtn.com/apps

Ave Maria Radio: https://avemariaradio.net/app/

Magnificat: https://us.magnificat.net/online

Relevant Radio: https://relevantradio.com/listen/get-the-app/

Discerning Hearts: https://www.discerninghearts.com/

iBreviary (Liturgy of the Hours and daily Mass readings):
https://www.ibreviary.org/en/

Hallow App: https://hallow.com/

Chaplets and Rosary: https://chaplets.us/

More Excellent Resources

For more Catholic and faith resources, visit Teresa Tomeo's resource page: https://teresatomeo.com/resources/.

About the Author

Teresa Tomeo is an author, syndicated Catholic talk-show host, and motivational speaker with more than thirty years of experience in TV, radio, and newspapers. She spent nineteen of those years working in front of a camera as a reporter and anchor in the Detroit market.

In 2000, Teresa left the secular media to start her own speaking and communications company, Teresa Tomeo Communications, LLC, and her website and blog (TeresaTomeo.com). Her daily morning radio program, *Catholic Connection*, is produced by Ave Maria Radio and EWTN's Global Catholic Radio Network and can be heard on more than five hundred domestic and international AM and FM radio affiliates worldwide, including SiriusXM Satellite Radio. Over the past two decades, Teresa has traveled extensively throughout Italy and has led numerous pilgrimages and tours there. In 2019, she founded *T's Italy*, a travel consultation company, along with its website (TravelItalyExpert.com), where she shares insider tips for where to eat, stay, shop, and play in that beautiful country.

Sophia Institute

Sophia Institute is a nonprofit institution that seeks to nurture the spiritual, moral, and cultural life of souls and to spread the gospel of Christ in conformity with the authentic teachings of the Roman Catholic Church.

Sophia Institute Press fulfills this mission by offering translations, reprints, and new publications that afford readers a rich source of the enduring wisdom of mankind.

Sophia Institute also operates the popular online resource CatholicExchange.com. *Catholic Exchange* provides world news from a Catholic perspective as well as daily devotionals and articles that will help readers to grow in holiness and live a life consistent with the teachings of the Church.

In 2013, Sophia Institute launched Sophia Institute for Teachers to renew and rebuild Catholic culture through service to Catholic education. With the goal of nurturing the spiritual, moral, and cultural life of souls, and an abiding respect for the role and work of teachers, we strive to provide materials and programs that are at once enlightening to the mind and ennobling to the heart; faithful and complete, as well as useful and practical.

Sophia Institute gratefully recognizes the Solidarity Association for preserving and encouraging the growth of our apostolate over the course of many years. Without their generous and timely support, this book would not be in your hands.

www.SophiaInstitute.com
www.CatholicExchange.com
www.SophiaInstituteforTeachers.org

Sophia Institute Press is a registered trademark of Sophia Institute.
Sophia Institute is a tax-exempt institution as defined by the
Internal Revenue Code, Section 501(c)(3). Tax ID 22-2548708.